SCHOOL MANAGEMENT
BY OBJECTIVES

James Lewis, Jr.

Parker Publishing Company, Inc.
West Nyack, New York

〰〰〰〰〰〰〰〰〰〰〰〰〰〰〰〰〰〰〰〰〰〰〰〰〰〰〰〰〰〰

To my mother—who died before this manuscript was completed

〰〰〰〰〰〰〰〰〰〰〰〰〰〰〰〰〰〰〰〰〰〰〰〰〰〰〰〰〰〰

©1974, by

PARKER PUBLISHING COMPANY, INC.
West Nyack, New York

Library of Congress Cataloging in Publication Data

Lewis, James,
    School management by objectives.

    Bibliography: p.
    1. School management and organization. I. Title.
LB2805.L42   371.2   74-5163
ISBN 0-13-793844-6

Printed in the United States of America

About the Author

Dr. James Lewis, Jr., is professor of education and chairman of the Division of Teacher Education at Medgar Evers College, a branch of the City University of New York. He also teaches in the Educational Administration Program at Villanova University. He holds a B.S. degree from Hampton Institute, an M.A. degree from Columbia University, and a Ph.D. degree from Union Graduate School, Antioch College. Dr. Lewis is a recipient of the Alfred North Whitehead Fellowship for Advanced Study in Education at Harvard University, awarded to established scholars and practitioners of distinction. He is President of the National Association for Individualization of Instruction and is the author of four earlier books: *A Contemporary Approach to Nongraded Education, Differentiating the Teaching Staff, Administering the Individualized Instruction Program,* and *Appraising Teacher Performance,* all published by Parker Publishing Company, Inc.

Foreword

School Management by Objectives represents a comprehensively defined attempt, on the part of the author, to provide the educational leader with a systemized approach to managing the urban educational program on the basis of clearly delineated objectives. Throughout the manuscript, Dr. James Lewis presents a series of procedures which, if implemented, enhance the educators' chances of installing a management system at the local school district level which will make a lasting and perhaps timely impact upon the way in which children learn in that setting. It is noted, for example, that Chapter 3 deals specifically with an identification of strategies designed to install the Management by Objectives process in the school setting. It includes considerations related to the establishment of long-range goals, an analysis of defined job descriptions, a review of results analysis, processes designed to enhance the development of individual improvement plans, and the procedures envisioned as pertaining to the establishment of training programs.

Additionally, as a part of the manuscript, the author identifies the process whereby the monitoring of performance as designed to secure improved results is accomplished. The goal-setting process is clearly identified, as well as the procedures which the educational administrator should follow as a means of establishing an action plan designed to achieve the predetermined objectives.

In the concluding portions of the work, Dr. Lewis reviews in some detail the psychological and sociological aspects of educational leadership, particularly as they pertain to such crucial components as student motivation, perception, needs assessment of children, leadership styles, reading for goals, teamsmanship in the administrative process, problem-solving and the decision-making process, and goal-setting sessions.

This is an age in which considerable interest has been placed upon the devising of models of accountability which will, in fact, guarantee that professional educaors are evaluated on the basis of the degree to which they are able to produce the results as defined in behavioral/performance objectives. The devising of an action plan which enables administration, in an organized manner, to get about the business of assisting staff in the developing of viable and meaningful goals which will lead to improved levels of achievement for kids is not an easy task.

The essential planning process is more than adequately described by the author in this book. It does not seek to provide the educational leader with a cookbook approach to "what do I do" as a means of guaranteeing the operationalizing of a fail-safe Management by Objectives model in a local school district. It does, however, describe some of the pitfalls which inevitably will be confronted by the educational leader who does seek to devise an operational model. Concurrently, it provides the reader with a series of step-by-step procedures which, if followed, can lead to success in the urban school setting. It is crucial to know in this regard that the Management by Objectives process cannot evolve in the absence of full commitment on the part of the superintendent and his executive staff. Hence the materials contained herein go far in the direction of providing that leadership with the kinds of concepts so vital to one's awareness of precisely how this important management system can be effectively established.

Dr. Edward B. Fort, Superintendent
Sacramento Public Schools
Sacramento, California

A Word from the Author
on the Value of MBO

This is a "what to do and how to do it" book. It deals with the organization of essential tasks educators must perform if they are determined to improve their schools. It organizes these tasks so that administrators, supervisors, and teachers can perform them systematically, purposefully, with understanding, and with reasonable assurance of success.

This book describes a relatively new process known as School Management by Objectives (School MBO). It identifies the philosophy, realistic concepts and specific approaches for determining what should be achieved in a school system and how to achieve it.

It is a practical rather than a theoretical book, and will help you improve overall school performance by demonstrating that accountability *can* become a reality in a school system regardless of its size and complexity. Through School MBO you will be able to give direction and purpose to the individual tasks of each educator on your school staff.

I believe this to be the first comprehensive and systematic plan for installing Management by Objectives in education. It will enable you to indentify key tasks, relate them to performance standards and develop mcthods for monitoring performance. In addition, this book will provide guidance for you to identify and cite problems in your school, set objectives and other plans to eliminate those problems. Here is a tested, successful approach toward a *discipline* for improving a school system.

There are 14 chapters which present the strategies, step-by-step, for implementing School MBO. Early chapters establish the fundamentals of the concept: the need for School MBO is substantiated and the system is fully identified.

Chapter 3 identifies the steps and overall strategy for installing the system. Chapters 4 through 7 deal with techniques for writing performance standards, methods of checking performance, highlighting development of long-range goals and short-range objectives, and establishment of a plan of action for achieving each objective. Chapter 8 describes the procedural steps for conducting the performance appraisal review. Chapters 9 and 10 show how to construct an Individual Improvement Guide for maintaining an acceptable level of performance, including School Department Improvement Plans and Individual Improvement Plans to insure superior performance. Chapter 11 illustrates the importance of training an advisor to oversee the School MBO program. Chapter 12 explains how to formulate an effective training program via School MBO. Chapter 13 identifies the key factors that make School MBO work: greater understanding and the application of motivational techniques. Chapter 14 covers frequently asked questions about School MBO and responds to these questions. The Appendix contains a sample Job Description, Individual Improvement Guide, School/Department Improvement Plan and Individual Improvement Plan.

This book is the direct result of experience as a chief school officer, knowledge gained at Harvard University and MIT, and numerous conferences held with noted experts in industry and education. All the approaches and programs have been tested and can be used effectively in either a small, medium or large school district. They can also be used individually, by teams or departments. There are charts, citations of problems and their solutions, illustrations, references to case histories and examples throughout the book, drawn from a variety of front-line educational experiences.

Because of its thorough coverage, unique features and relevance to contemporary problems in public and private school systems, this book will be valuable to a wide variety of school-related personnel: superintendents, supervisors, principals, teachers, board members, parents and college faculty. It will offer special value to seasoned administrators who desire to improve and refine the skills necessary in identifying and *achieving* important educational objectives.

James Lewis, Jr.

ACKNOWLEDGMENTS

It is a pleasure for me to acknowledge the help of many people. My gratitude to Edith Reisner, librarian at the Wyandanch School District, Wyandanch, New York, for the critical reading and editing of this manuscript. I am also appreciative of the assistance afforded me by Joan Schorr, who developed professionally the charts and graphs for this manuscript, and by Caroline Allen and Dorothy Mattison, who painstakingly deciphered my difficult penmanship and labored many hours typing this book.

I am especially indebted, in many different ways, to the writings of the late Douglas McGregor, Charles L. Hughes, John W. Humble, M. Scott Myers and George S. Odiorne, and to the thoughts of A. Gordon Peterkin and Stan Newman.

I am also thankful to God for giving me the strength to continue giving birth to words and ideas for the improvement of education in this country.

Table of Contents

ONE

Identifying the Needs for School Management by Objectives

School districts that have implemented Management by Objectives (MBO) have done so out of the desire to find an effective professional appraisal and development program. This has often resulted in disenchantment with the traditional methods of operating the school. Business firms, schools and departments that have installed the system quickly learned that Management by Objectives also served other useful purposes.

School MBO is so constituted as to serve several purposes at the same time in the efficient operation of the schools. It can be used to:

- effectuate an effective school planning program,
- increase the control and coordination of people and activities,
- maximize proper utilization of personnel,
- install more effective methods for appraising performance, and
- initiate an improved training and development program.

This chapter is concerned with citing problems inherent to the present traditional school program and it will explain how School MBO can be used to alleviate these conditions.

MORE EFFECTIVE SCHOOL PLANNING PROGRAM

Most public schools do not have a systematic approach either to short- or long-range planning.

While most schools have established broad educational objectives, few schools have translated these objectives into specific goals and objectives which apply at all levels of school management. It is not enough for a school district to state that its goal is to provide opportunities for each child to progress in school according to his individual abilities, interest levels, rate of speed and talents. Unless this broad educational objective is translated into actual assignments in terms of long-range goals and specific short-range objectives, it will be mere chance if the broad objective is ever reached. The final result to be achieved is actually the purpose of the objective. The means must still be provided in order to determine how the school personnel will generate alternatives. Possible alternatives could be the nongraded concept, differentiated staffing, behavioral objective program, computer assisted instruction, team teaching, or a systems approach to instruction.

Let us say that the alternative strategy which was selected and mutually agreed upon by the board of education and school personnel was differentiated staffing (long-range goal). The business manager and the school planning committee must agree on the specific objectives for computing salary differentials. The assistant superintendent in charge of personnel and the planning committee must agree on specific objectives in view of personnel needs. The assistant superintendent of curriculum and instruction is concerned with the academic program; he and his staff must set specific objectives in this area. Building principals and their staffs must then develop objectives. Finally, each classroom teacher must identify specific objectives.

In order to achieve the broad educational objective and to provide opportunities for each child to progress according to his individual ability, interest levels, rate of speed and talents, the results (in terms of specific objectives) to be achieved in every part of the school must be spelled out in advance. The school district then has a comprehensive plan reached by mutual agreement between those who will perform the tasks. Add the action plan and the timetable and the school district will have programmed its action tasks for the period in question.

The period of time may be short range (usually one year) or long range (any range which is over a duration of three years). Long-range goals and short-range objectives are discussed in detail in Chapter 6.

Item:

A Connecticut school district has been using School MBO for three years. While the program was installed primarily to establish a planning system, a results orientation built into the system emphasizes the importance of individual administrators' actions and decisions. Using long-range goals established by the board of education and the superintendent, each administrator establishes short-range objectives and action plans directed toward achieving long-range goals. Each administrator is appraised semi-annually by his immediate supervisor. The Master Plan for operating the school district consists of the long-range goals, short-range objectives and action plans. In this school district, MBO is a vehicle for performance appraisal as well as school operations planning. At first, the program was implemented for central administration only; after the second year, the program applied to the individual schools within the district. Now there is an administrator who reports directly to the superintendent with respect to his responsibility for administering the present program and developing plans to apply MBO to the entire school district.

Planning may be the most important benefit from the School MBO program. Effective planning leads to better time utilization, reduces the incidence of trial and error, leads to more rational work assignment, and provides opportunities for better utilization of scarce resources.

INCREASED CONTROL AND COORDINATION

There is very little systematic control and coordination in the operation of day-to-day affairs in the public schools.

The implementation of School MBO provides a system by which control of the school is determined by the progress of all of its activities. This control may take various forms: PPBS, academic achievement test results, statistical records, Individual Improvement Guides, School/Department Improvement Plans, performance appraisal review report and others. Effective school management control techniques are supported by some definite objectives or standards against which performance will be measured.

In the absence of well-defined objectives it would be rather difficult to establish any sort of control over the broad educational objectives of the program. School MBO not only establishes necessary specific objectives, but in so doing, also establishes its own system of control. When objectives have been mutually agreed upon, checking is simply accomplished by comparing the results achieved against the desired results.

The process of coordination, which is very important to the success of a school, is maintained as a result of the achievement of specific objectives at each level of operation. The goal which requires the implementation of differentiated staffing sets off a chain of necessary coordinations. The federal aid coordinator may be required to develop a proposal for the implementation of the differentiated staffing. The assistant superintendent in charge of personnel may be required to recruit intern teachers to fill a slot in the differentiated staffing pattern. The directors of elementary and secondary education may be required to retain the services of consultants to assist in the retraining of teachers. In essence, each educator involved in the implementation of differentiated staffing must coordinate his activities with those of every other person. Target dates for the achievement of specific objectives must be set and met in a coordinated effort for reaching the broad educational objectives. School MBO helps to establish and maintain coordination and makes certain that the necessary target dates have been established.

MAXIMUM UTILIZATION OF SCHOOL PERSONNEL

Because specific objectives have not been identified through the traditional method of operating our public schools, there is a duplication of effort resulting in a waste in staff utilization.

The effectiveness of the school personnel is directly proportionate to the degree to which each person's effort is directed. Without this direction, a great deal of sincere effort is likely to be wasted.

A school district's effectiveness is impaired when specific objectives have not been delineated and educators pursue unclear objectives. When School MBO is implemented, control, coordination and evaluation come into play, a continuous improvement in the activities of the school and more effective utilization of school personnel are almost certain to result. This more efficient method of operating a school provides opportunities for an administrator to check on staff directly and to recommend continuous activities for personal development. When all school personnel are oriented to the long-range goals of the school through their specific objectives, greater efficiency can be maintained by more effective staff utilization.

MORE EFFECTIVE METHOD FOR APPRAISING PERFORMANCE

The need for an effective method or instrument for evaluating the performance of school personnel has been a problem which has perplexed educators for years.

Traditionally the evaluation of teachers, supervisors and administrators has been more or less subjective and inept. Emphasis tends to be placed on effort expended rather than on results achieved.

The professional evaluation terms and procedures presently being used in most schools are designed to rate school personnel according to factors which measure overall effectiveness. Some of these factors are: class participation, voice control, display of initiative, knowledge of subject matter, health and cleanliness, etc. These factors are at best poor yardsticks for measuring performance because they do not measure results, and results determine, to a large extent, the success of the educators and thus ultimately of the school. For

371. 2 L5872s

example, an administrator or teacher may be knowledgeable about his job, be in good health, get along well with others, and yet not produce in terms of job performance.

An examination of traditional professional evaluation forms will reveal that schools have attempted to use them for the purpose of measuring educators' performances without a clear idea of what they want to measure. As an illustration, let us examine the evaluation form of a school district and select one of the criteria for determining "professional effectiveness." At the top portion of the form the terms "poor," "fair," "good," "excellent," and "superior" are used to designate the evaluator's estimate of performance success. A number of points are enumerated at the left margin of the form, denoting various criteria for assessing performance. One criterion states: "The teacher is conscious of the individuality of each student." The farce about this type of performance appraisal form stems from the fact that the terms "poor," "fair," "good," etc., are subjective terms; what may be *fair* to some may be *poor* to others, and so on.

Item:

> Although Management by Objectives is relatively new in education, the program has been implemented in a number of schools throughout the nation. In one midwestern school district the program was introduced primarily as a more effective process for appraising teachers' performances and helping teachers to improve their skills and abilities. Some administrators objected initially to their "new" role as a staff developer; however, this objection was only temporary. This school district found that teachers were unable to write meaningful objectives unless the central administration office transmitted its long-range goals throughout the school district. This same school district found that School MBO helped administrators to identify problems in the system which had gone unattended for years. There was also a noticeable improvement in staff development.

Perhaps the greatest benefit to be derived from School MBO is the decreased need for close supervision of personnel. Teachers—or all educators, for that matter—participate fully in arriving at performance objectives and action plans. Although there may be some changes in the initial proposed objectives and action plans when they are discussed with the administrator, the final package is arrived at by mutual agreement. Some administrators have stated that through this managerial process they have had an improved method for discussing individual performance. A noticeable change is also seen in the warm relationship which is generated between the administrator and the teacher during the latter's performance appraisal review.

In the past the evaluation session between the teacher and the administrator was something of a fiasco. The administrator played the role of a top boss and made a series of judgments about the teacher's performance, usually sandwiching each "bad" remark between two "good" remarks.

Under School MBO, the "conference" session replaces the "evaluation" session; the teacher's performance review becomes a matter in which the educator and his immediate supervisor play equal roles in improving performance. Both know what the performance objectives and action plans are, both have the same information about the actual results achieved, and both use the same measures for comparing the projected objectives with the results achieved.

BETTER TRAINING AND DEVELOPMENT PROGRAM

The training and development programs found in most traditional schools which consist of in-service courses bear little or no relation to the problems found on the job.

School MBO is an invaluable means for improving training and development programs. This is achieved in several ways.

Mutually agreed-upon specific objectives are a matter of personal accountability. In essence, every school person is forced to stand on his own two feet. This prevents personality catering, passing the buck, or job skipping.

Because School MBO provides an accurate means for measuring personnel performance, personal strengths and weaknesses are easily identifiable. Therefore additional training can quickly be provided. By isolating specific individual weaknesses, the school district can adopt an individualized approach to improving the performance of its members. After observing the individual progress of each person in his effort to achieve his specific objectives, it is possible for the school district to maintain a detailed record of the school personnel's strengths and weaknesses. It is also possible for all of the strengths to be lumped together for the primary purpose of exposing a faculty or a group of educators to a general developmental training program. The school district officials can also prescribe and conduct special training programs for members who may need them. The following is a description of how the system of School MBO operates with respect to training and development.

At the beginning of the school year, specific objectives are mutually agreed to by the administrator and each staff member. The objectives which are related to the staff members' job responsibilities are then developed into Individual Improvement Plans. A first draft of these plans is usually prepared by each staff member and then mutually agreed to in a conference or negotiation session between the administrator and his staff members. Changes may or may not result. If there are changes, they are mutually agreed to. The personal development objectives may have been prescribed by the administrator, or based on his prior assessment of performance. Once all objectives have been mutually agreed to, the improvement plans are paramount.

Periodically and at the end of the school year, the administrator and each staff member will discuss which objectives were achieved and which were not. A performance appraisal review session contributes to the climate of understanding at such sessions. How well the objectives were achieved, what limitations and constraints prevented the achievement of the objectives, and what objectives were not achieved as planned will be discussed. The performance appraisal review session should involve only the achievement of specific objectives relative to the job assignment. This session should be a frank, open discussion; it should never be used for the purpose of reprimanding an educator who did not make a satisfactory achievement. The conference should be performed in a professional manner which permits free exchange of opinions. The performance appraisal review session should never be conducted in an atmosphere of fear or skepticism. The discussion during the session becomes one in which notes are compared and progress is reviewed. The administrator and the staff members discuss the job, the methods for improving it, and the results to be achieved.

Item:

> A medium-sized school district located in the Midwest began its School MBO program four years ago. Implementation was on a gradual basis, starting with the central administration staff and later including building principals. Performance objectives are set for 6- and 12-month durations. The school district uses the program as a basis for appraising administrators' performance and developing a training and development program. School MBO is regarded as a major contribution to the school district's improvement program which is designed to improve administrators' performance, thereby improving teachers' performance, and ultimately students' performance.

School MBO provides a systematic means of tailoring the training and development program to the individual needs of each school person. Furthermore, it supplies a built-in provision for self-appraisal and self-renewal, without which a school system cannot survive—and with which a school system becomes dynamic.

IDENTIFYING PROBLEMS ASSOCIATED WITH SCHOOL MBO

It would be unfair for the author to list the advantages of School MBO without indicating some of the problems or disadvantages.

Requires Hard Work

Perhaps most of the problems are summed up under one heading—*hard work*. Good things don't come in easy packages; this is certainly true for School MBO and particularly true for educators. School administration was usually performed according to two inept methods: "seat-of-the-pants" administration and "top-of-the-head" administration. It is now time to give way to a proven and effective method of operating the schools through the systematic process of School MBO. This will require hard work and will necessitate undoing some things and making adjustments to a more effective method of doing things. For this reason, School MBO should be seen as a long-range effort to get maximum benefits.

Needs Time to Apply

Although the concept of School MBO is a logical and systematic process, many educators have a difficult time learning how to apply the concept. It will probably take administrators and supervisors two to three years before they are truly proficient in implementing the concept. For educators, most problems occur when developing performance objectives, applying effective motivation techniques, and initiating proper coaching and counseling methods.

Not a Panacea

Although School MBO does have an umbrella effect—that is, it can be used to improve a number of areas within a school district—it is not a panacea. A procedure that may work best for one area may not necessarily be appropriate in another.

Initiation Problem

School MBO tends to be more successful when the chief school officer is committed to the concept and is the initiator thereof. When the program has been initiated by educators who are of low status or low competence, or whose educational leadership is questionable, gaining acceptance for the program will be difficult.

Old Ways Are Difficult to Erase

Poor administration practices and unsound organizational patterns tend to have a contaminating effect on educators. School MBO must assume a decontaminating role which sometimes is either impossible or extremely difficult to do.

Emphasis on Procedure

School MBO has failed to make an appreciable difference in some school districts mainly because some administrators have been known to implement the procedure rather than the substance. To add substance to the program, there must be a commitment on the part of top administrators to follow through on the program efforts made by administrators and supervisors to motivate, coach and counsel for improved performance.

Beating the System

If the supervisor does not require the substantiation of "on" or "above" performance, an educator may be able to beat the system by recording untrue performance reports.

SUMMARY

School MBO is useful in the following ways: it provides a means for systematically conducting long- and short-range planning; it improves control and coordination in the school by keeping check (periodic and annual) on all the activities of the school; it makes for maximum utilization of school personnel through the distribution of specific performance objectives; it assures equitable distribution of time, work load and compensation through the review of job performance; it establishes a more effective method for appraising the performance of school personnel by the objective nature of the specific performance objectives; and it fosters better training development programs through workshops or personal development objectives.

Some of the problems associated with School MBO are: (1) it requires hard work; (2) it needs time to apply; (3) it is not a panacea; (4) there is an initiation problem; (5) old ways are difficult to erase; (6) emphasis on procedure; (7) educators may be able to beat the system.

TWO

Understanding the System of School Management by Objectives

When objectives are specifically and clearly defined, a school can be managed more effectively. School MBO can be achieved only when it is preceded by an organized method of setting goals. Initially, goals are established by the board of education and superintendent and sequentially phased into or integrated with goals developed by various other professional personnel within the school system. During conferences between the educator and his immediate supervisor, the former has an opportunity to participate in the development of his own goals, objectives and plan of action for improving his performance. Thus, the system of School MBO is based essentially upon an orderly arrival at mutually agreed-upon goals.

The purpose of this chapter is to define school management, present the basic conditions of school management, focus on the functions of school management, relate objectives to school management, define School MBO, discuss a systems approach to management (School MBO), and explain how educational accountability is ensured.

DEFINING SCHOOL MANAGEMENT

School management is a process of utilizing human resources for the effective operation of schools. It is people-oriented in every sense of the word, because it deals primarily with the development of *human beings* and does not deal with the direction of *things*.

In the operation of a public school, every professional person is a manager. The involvement of all educators in planning and controlling as well as in task performance is accepted not as a good gesture or a means of exploitation but rather as good school practice. Benefits accrue to the school system in terms of knowledgeable and competent teachers, supervisors and administrators. Ultimately, each individual grows and develops within the school setting.

BASIC CONDITIONS OF SCHOOL MANAGEMENT

Effective school management depends upon practices which follow four basic principles:

1. *Decentralization of Staff Members*

Most school districts are too large (even the smallest of them) for direct management. Complete authority and responsibility must be delegated within the framework of adopted policies of the school.

2. *Maintaining Accountability*

School personnel must be held accountable to immediate supervisors for performance of mutually agreed-upon goals and objectives according to their delegated authority and responsibility.

3. *Development and Growth of School Personnel*

Development and growth of school related personnel is an individual and collective responsibility. Each and every school person is responsible for his individual growth and development. School administrators are responsible for creating a climate for personal growth and development. Administrators and supervisors are responsible for the growth and development of their staff members.

4. *Personnel Involvement*

School MBO involves the interaction of school personnel in the processes of development, decision-making, planning and organizing, performing and evaluating. This is particularly true when the individuals involved will be affected by what is being accomplished. Another positive aspect of personnel involvement is that each individual has the ability to contribute. In a democratic society, involvement is one of the most important principles of effective school management.

THE FUNCTION OF SCHOOL MANAGEMENT

There are two main functions of school management. Within these functions are sub-functions which, when properly executed, immensely improve the school's operation.

Planning

The first function of school management is that of *planning*. This process encompasses the entire field of educating children. It is the process of assigning job duties to school personnel. Primarily, planning involves:

1. The determination of priorities for effective operation. Needs priorities should be determined with maximum personnel involvement, including board members, school personnel, members of the community, and students.
2. The establishment of objectives in order to provide both the guidelines for individual performance and the means to assess performance.
3. The formulation of a procedure by which objectives will be set and achieved, and performance reviewed.
4. The assignment of responsibility to individuals or groups so that accountability can be ascertained.

Control

The second function of school management is that of *control*. This process requires the use of various methods and techniques to impel educators to perform in accordance with their objectives. Factors which can enhance control are:

1. Maintaining an organized structure and keeping it as simple as possible to avoid confusion and misunderstanding.
2. Maintaining adequate supervision to seal gaps in the school system which reflect performance delay.
3. Maintaining accurate information in order to make decisions and assess performance.

Administrators and supervisors must be able to determine the performance tasks their staff are to achieve, select the most qualified personnel to accomplish these tasks, check periodically to ascertain how well each member is performing, and develop techniques and methods which help each educator to improve his performance.

The following statement by Lawrence A. Appley is not only apropos for business, but can be equally well applied in education:

TEN COMMANDMENTS OF MANAGEMENT

1. Identify the people of an organization as its greatest asset.
2. Make profit, in order to continue rendering service. [In education this statement pertains to improving student performance for survivability.]
3. Approach every task in an organized, conscious manner so that the outcome will not be left to chance.
4. Establish definite long- and short-range objectives to insure greater accomplishment.
5. Secure full attainment of objectives through general understanding and acceptance of them by others.
6. Keep individual members of the team well adjusted by seeing that each knows what he is supposed to do, how well he is supposed to do it, what his authority is, and what his work relationships with others should be.
7. Concentrate on individual improvement through regular review of performance and potential.
8. Provide opportunity for assistance and guidance in self-development as a fundamental of institutional growth.
9. Maintain adequate and timely incentives and rewards for increase in effort.
10. Supply work satisfactions for those who perform the work and those who are served by it.[1]

RELATING OBJECTIVES TO SCHOOL MANAGEMENT

In order to develop a modern managerial philosophy that will lend itself to successful practices in the operation of American schools, a combination of objectives is required. Specific performance objectives must be developed and mutually agreed to by the parties concerned; without them there can be little or no real basis for measuring the effectiveness of anyone who performs in our schools.

The formulation of a school management principle is the result of pre-

---

[1]Lawrence A. Appley, "The Management Evolution," American Management Association: New York, N.Y., 1965.

determining goals and objectives. Before initiating any effort, the goal or objective must be determined, clearly stated, and understood. Relating objectives to school management means specifically that the administrator must:

1. *Plan* to achieve predetermined goals and objectives.
2. *Organize* the structure to initiate the required action and to achieve the objective.
3. *Motivate* staff to accomplish the objective.
4. *Control* the effort for objective attainment.
5. *Use* performance as a basis of training and developing staff.

The concept of School MBO is derived when objectives relate to school management. The concept as a whole, whether applied at school, department or individual level, is based on the premise that ". . . unless you know where you want to go you are unlikely to get there, and unless you know what results you want you are unlikely to achieve them."[2]

DEFINING SCHOOL MANAGEMENT BY OBJECTIVES

The system of School MBO involves more than a set of rules, a series of procedures, or even a firm method for administrating schools and managing personnel. School MBO is a philosophical approach; it is a way of thinking about operating American schools. It is a *process* whereby all school personnel identify their common and uncommon goals as a basis for defining successful criteria for evaluating the degree of goal attainment. These measures are then used to ascertain the degree of effectiveness of each educator and to judge the extent of accountability of our schools in terms of increased student performance. School MBO is essentially a system of constructing school operations into a logical and effective pattern. The value of systematic School MBO can be noticed in tangible areas such as increased student performance, more effective utilization of school personnel, improved methods and techniques and more happy and contented parents. On the intangible side, School MBO enhances the operations of the schools by affecting quality, school personnel performance, research opportunities and students' growth. Additional effects include better morale, increased trust among the faculty, effective communication network, improved quality of school personnel, effective system for assessing overall growth and improved method for making important decisions.

---

[2]Lesley Bernstein, *Management Development,* Business Book Ltd.: London, England, 1968, p. 21.

As in the nongraded philosophy,[3] it is a way of thinking about operating American schools and managing the human beings who service those schools.

Item:

A school district in California attributes much of the success of its School MBO program to the fact that if a teacher or administrator sets his own performance objectives and develops his own plan for achieving his objectives, he will be more inclined to achieve them and will have a greater sense of accountability. Performance objectives are set for a one-year period and are reviewed every 20 weeks. Each teacher and administrator is required to set four performance objectives. Each objective will include an action plan and must be approved by the immediate supervisor. Most objectives center around the implementation of new methods and procedures, increased attendance, and improvement in academic programs.

The author elaborates on the conceptual framework of the school organization by paraphrasing the text of George S. Odiorne, the originator of Management by Objectives.

1. The basic structure of the school is an organizational form called the line of authority. This is the familiar arrangement of hierarchical boxes displaying the board of education at the top box, the superintendent immediately beneath the top box with the appropriate number of subordinate boxes in successive levels. School MBO is a means or system for making this system work, putting accountability in motion and producing more vitality and personal involvement of school personnel in the hierarchy.

2. School MBO provides for the continuous and orderly growth of the school system by means, first, of clearly delineated statements of goals for each person involved in the operation of the schools and then measuring what is achieved in relation to the objectives. It assigns and distributes management risk to all responsible school officials, administrators, supervisors, specialists, teachers and related nonprofessional service personnel and makes their progress and job survival dependent upon demonstrated production. It stresses judging all school personnel on the basis of ability and achievement rather than on individual personalities.

3. School MBO helps overcome many critical problems associated with managing school personnel; for example:

   a. It provides an accurate means by which the individual school person's contributions can be measured and evaluated in terms of his role and responsibilities in relation to the total operation of the schools.

---

[3]James Lewis, Jr., *A Contemporary Approach to Nongraded Education,* Parker Publishing Company, Inc., West Nyack, N.Y., 1969.

b. It defines the common and unique goals of the various school personnel within the school organization and measures how each individual contributes to goals, thereby enhancing the opportunities for coordination, articulation and teamwork without diminishing personal risk.

c. It provides for total involvement in terms of arriving at goals of the school, thereby helping to nurture trust among the school personnel and staff members.

d. It helps solve important problems within the school by defining the major areas of responsibility for each person in the school, including individual and shared responsibilities.

e. It is a system geared to achieving results for which the schools were originally intended.

f. It eliminates "personality catering" in order to receive favorable performance evaluation reports; focus is on results achieved.

g. It is a means by which the span of control of each school is personally identified.

h. It *can be* used as an accountability guide allocating pay increases for obtained results.

i. It aids in identifying school personnel for firing, advancing and promoting.

j. It systematically isolates problem areas for concentrating efforts to determine means to control and resolvement.

4. Because School MBO is a system, it is applicable to professionals and nonprofessionals. It can and should extend from the board of education to part-time employees.[4]

School MBO may also be defined as a method of operating the school district which permits educators to concentrate on those activities requiring close attention. If educators establish objectives and periodically measure results, they can give maximum attention to those objectives which are "off target" and can take corrective actions to get "on target." Without such a warning system, educators may spend too much time and energy on trivial matters and too little time and energy on important matters. Obviously, nothing much would be achieved.

One of the best definitions of School MBO was stated by Harlow H. Curtice, in his statement before the subcommittee on Anti-Trust and Monopoly of the U. S. Senate Committee on Judiciary, December 2, 1955:

---

[4]George S. Odiorne, *Management by Objectives – A System of Managerial Leadership*, Pitman Publishing Corp., New York, N.Y., 1965, pp. 54-55.

It is really an attitude of mind. It might be defined as bringing the research point of view to bear on all phases of the *school district*. This involves, first, assembling all the facts; second, analysis of where the facts appear to point; and third, courage to follow the trail indicated even if it leads into unfamiliar and unexplored territory. This point of view is never satisfied with things as they are.[5]

In the subsequent chapters of this manuscript the author will relate the concept of MBO to public and private education. He will perform this task by considering the concept as a method of orienting the performance of all educators at all levels to the philosophy of the school district and to the personal goals of the individual performer to ensure that the goals and the objectives are achieved in the most appropriate manner with a minimum of time and effort. The reader should be able to determine that School MBO is a highly rewarding and effective system which offers the greatest opportunity in terms of educational growth of youngsters. This is the ultimate mission of any school system.

SYSTEMS APPROACH TO MANAGEMENT: SCHOOL MANAGEMENT BY OBJECTIVES

It should also be stressed by the author that School MBO is not a technique or procedure that sounds good in theory but which has not been tried and proven. We have only to witness the successes of industrial and business firms. A number of school districts are using objectives in the management of their offices with a great deal of success on the part of all parties concerned.

Is it valid to a school? Is School MBO really a systems approach? When an organization such as a school is said to function as a system, it means that the school or school districts "consist of a number of components, with each component differentiated from each other in terms of particular functions to be performed and that all of these functions contribute in some way to the accomplishment of the organization's purpose. Further, the term *system* implies that the relationships among the various components are characterized by interdependence, regularity, order and predictability."[6]

---

[5]The author has substituted the words "school district" for "business" in the original text of Harlow H. Curtice.

[6]Max G. Abbott and Terry L. Eidell, "Administration Implementation of Curriculum Performance," *Educational Technology*, May, 1970, pp. 62-64.

School MBO *should not:*

- Be overcomplicated and overcomplicate the function of a school administrator and supervisor, but should simplify as much as humanly possible a job that has become extremely burdened with data, method, techniques and procedures.
- Be dominated by its mechanics or by hard-set rules or guides to be strictly adhered to.
- Be so philosophical and speculative that its effects are beyond measurement. Measurement of results is important because parents are demanding that the school give clear evidence of student performance and progress.
- Be impossible for school administrators to use without having to lean on other school personnel every step of the way.
- Require heavy inputs of fear, control, or directions from the top echelon into lower echolons, but should be self-regulating and self-operating.[7]

School MBO is not a complex system. The first requirement of the system is that it simplify and add meaning to the overwhelming masses of school-related information. How necessary this is for today's school personnel is evident from the terminology that assaults them on all sides—motivation; reinforcement; cognitive, affective and psychomotor domains; learning option; community relations; computer assisted instruction; differentiated staffing; non-graded philosophy; educational technology; and literally hundreds of other terms within a system that classifies and demonstrates the input and output effects of these words. It is impossible to make sense, let alone practical use of all this information.

The major focus of what School MBO can do successfully is as follows:

1. School management takes place within the educational complex that provides the environmental setting and situation for the education of youngsters. This complex and the environment have not been successful in the education of all youngsters. The community, an integral part of the educational complex, is imposing new requirements on the students and the individual school personnel.

2. School MBO is a new way of administration aimed at meeting new requirements. It presumes that the initial step in school management is to identify, by one means or another, the goals and objectives of the school district. All other management methods and sub-systems are subordinated to this preliminary step.

---

[7]George S. Odiorne, *Management by Objectives,* Pitman Publishing Corp., New York, 1965, pp. VI-VII.

3. Once the goals and objectives have been identified, procedures for assigning responsibilities among individual school personnel members are established in such a way that their combined and concentrated efforts are directed toward achieving the goals of the school.

4. School MBO assumes that school personnel performance or behavior is more important than the personality of individuals and that the performance or behavior should be identified in terms of results measured against established goals or objectives. What is practiced today in most American schools is in terms of common goals for all school personnel or the role of general practitioners on all levels of the echelons with not much concrete result.

5. School MBO also presumes that while participation in goals or performance-setting and decision-making is highly desirable, its principal merit rests in its social and practical value rather than in its efforts in the educational program. However, its primary intent is to make a profound effect on the education of youngsters.

6. School MBO regards successful administration and supervisors as managers or social engineers of situations, most of which are best defined by identifying the rationales of the school organization and the performance or behavior best calculated to achieve that purpose. This means that there is no one prescription for school management, since all behavior or performance is discriminating and each is related to specific goals or objectives and further shaped by the larger institutional system of the school within which it operates.

7. The utilization of objectives in school management helps to establish trust among all levels of school management because all school personnel involved are aware of their unique roles and specific responsibilities.

8. School MBO provides a basic framework from which accountability is easily identifiable.

9. School MBO leads the way for better techniques, methods and procedures to be introduced into the educational programs without suspicion, fear or reluctance because of the total and committed involvement which this process engenders.[8]

ENSURING EDUCATIONAL ACCOUNTABILITY

Educational accountability is the process by which teachers, supervisors and administrators are held responsible for the improvement or lack of improvement in the performance of students. There is nothing especially new in

---

[8]Ibid, pp. VII-VIIII.

the concept of responsibility in education; educators have always been concerned about improving the performance of students. What is new is the means by which educational accountability is ensured to satisfy a heightened awareness of responsibility for performance as well as the higher level of expectation. When School MBO is implemented properly, educational accountability is ensured through the following processes:

Mutual Agreement on Improvement Guides and Plans

The improvement guides and plans are mutually agreed to by the educator and his supervisor and become a contract between said parties. Both parties are equally responsible for the desired results as covered in the guide and plans. Thus, results achieved are dependent upon mutual cooperation, trust and assistance.

Monitoring of Performance

It is equally important for the educator as well as his supervisor to know if the desired result will be achieved as planned. When performance is properly monitored, corrective action can be taken to achieve the projected results if necessary.

Master Plan for School District-Wide Improvement

The accumulation of all improvement guides and plans becomes the master plan for ensuring educational accountability for the school district.

Issuance of Educational Accountability Report

The superintendent, assisted by the School MBO advisor, uses the results achieved and recorded on the improvement plans to plan, develop and distribute an annual educational accountability report to the board of education, staff, students and parents. This report is similar to the one submitted to stockholders by corporations.

Program Financing (PPBS)

Program planning and budget systems (PPBS) is a process for ensuring accountability through program financing. PPBS can easily be facilitated when MBO is properly installed in a school system.

Substantiation of Performance

It is the responsibility of the individual educator to substaniate on- and above-plan performance through any means deemed acceptable by the supervisor. In this way subjectivity is minimized and objectivity is maximized.

Technique for Establishing Training Needs

Traditional in-service education courses have proved disappointing for two reasons: (1) they were often viewed as activities separate from the real job, and (2) supervisors tended to concentrate on an educator's traits and personality instead of on results achieved. A more effective training program is devised when actual performance is assessed. When the gap between actual and desired performance is identified, a training program can be tailored to fill specific needs.

Review of Results and Necessary Action Taken

Using improvement guides and plans and supported by relevant information, performance is reviewed periodically. The performance review covers:

1. A review of performance achieved against the agreed objectives.
2. An analysis of variances.
3. Action required to effect improvement.
4. The revision of objectives if necessary.
5. The revision or development of new improvement plans, when and if necessary.

LEVELS OF JOB PERFORMANCE AND STAGES
OF EDUCATIONAL ACCOUNTABILITY

There are basically three levels of job performance: (1) actual performance level, (2) minimal performance level, and (3) aspirational performance level.

School districts which have not implemented School MBO are maintaining an actual performance level which does not meet performance requirements as set forth by the job description. This has resulted primarily because the mere completion of a job description is insufficient to maintain minimal performance. In many school districts across the nation, the job description is seldom referred to, becomes outdated, and often can be located in a far corner of a desk drawer accumulating dust.

Parents have become conscious of the actual performance level in our schools because there is a lack of accountability which has resulted because of the following:

1. Key areas are not identified.
2. No standards of performance have been matched with key areas of responsibility.
3. Methods of checking performance have not been stated.
4. There has been no assessment of strengths and weaknesses to arrive at needs.
5. Goals and objectives have not been set.
6. No action plans have been developed to attain objectives.
7. Behavioral theories have not been applied to improve performance.
8. No training program has been derived from performance weaknesses.

To maintain a minimal performance level, all educators within a school district are required to conduct a key results analysis, that is, they are required to use the job description as a basis for segmentizing key areas of responsibilities, match performance standards with these key areas, and establish methods for checking performance. When these activities have been completed, a condition of educational accountability is maintained in the school district which is identified as minimal accountability level.

The aspirational performance level results when the minimal performance level is sustained, problems and needs have been cited, goals and objectives are set and attained through action plans, performance has been reviewed, and motivation applied to improve performance. When these conditions have been met, we have achieved an educational accountability level described as maximum accountability level. An ultimate educational accountability level is never really achieved.

SUMMARY

School management is defined as the process of utilizing human resources for the effective operation of the schools. The basic conditions of school management consist of four items: (1) Decentralization of Staff—for the purpose of assigning authority and responsibility for the operations of the school; (2) Accountability—holding school personnel accountable to their immediate supervisors; (3) Development and Growth of School Personnel—in order to improve the performance of school personnel; (4) Personnel Involvement—for getting results by total participation and involvement.

The primary functions of school management are to *plan* by the participatory decision-making process the tasks to be performed, to *control* the use of various methods and techniques, and to *lead* school personnel to perform in accordance with their aspirations. School MBO is the process whereby all school personnel identify their common and unique goals, define their individual responsibility for achieving their goals, and determine the success criteria.

Relating objectives to school management means specifically that the administrator must: (1) plan to achieve predetermined goals and objectives; (2) organize the structure to initiate the required action to achieve the objective; (3) motivate staff to accomplish the objectives; (4) control the exerted effort for objective attainment; (5) use performance as a basis of training and developing staff.

School MBO involves more than a set of rules, a series of procedures, or even a firm method for administering schools and supervising personnel. School MBO is a philosophical approach and, similar to the non-graded philosophy, it is a way of thinking about operating American schools and humanizing the human beings who service those schools. When School MBO is implemented properly, educational accountability is ensured through: mutual agreement on improvement guides and plans, monitoring performance, master plan for school-district-wide improvement, issuance of educational accountability report, program financing, substantiating performance, identifying a technique for establishing training needs, reviewing results and measuring action tasks. There are basically three levels of job performance: (1) actual performance, (2) minimal performance level, and (3) aspirational performance level.

THREE

Installing the System of School Management by Objectives

If the author were to leave the reader with only one important message about the installation of School Management by Objectives, that message would evolve around the importance of careful and methodical planning action before, during, and after the concept has been initiated. (See Figure 3-1.) All educators must be convinced that the management approach to be installed in the school district is to aid them in improving their individual and collective performance, thereby raising the performance level of the entire school system, not to create additional work for them, not to seek a method to dismiss them, and certainly not to confuse them with a useful but complicated procedure.

The purpose of this chapter is to delineate the preliminary steps for installing School MBO, to outline the installment procedures, to identify a strategy for installing School MBO, to discuss the final stage—reporting results, and to identify problems associated with the implementation of School MBO and some solutions to these conditions.

PRELIMINARY STEPS

Obtain Commitment from Top Administrators

School MBO must have the complete support and backing of the chief school officer. This commitment must also extend to the central administration. All educators must be convinced of the value of their supervisor's plan to manage the school district through a systematic Management by Objectives

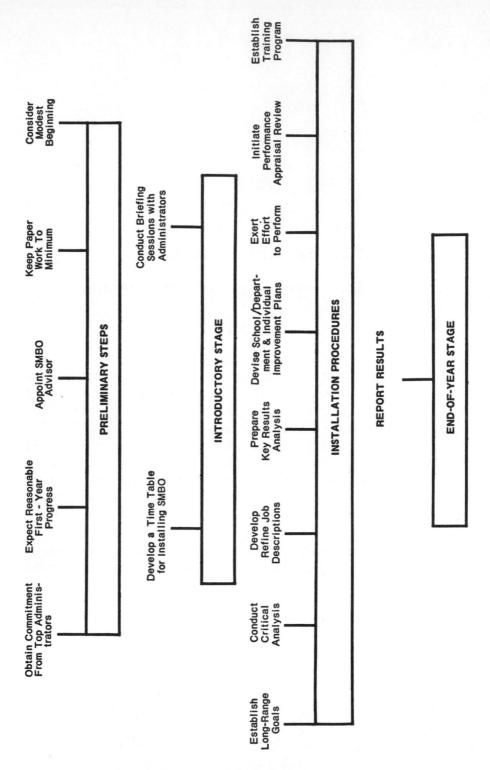

FIGURE 3-1
Installing the System of School Management by Objectives

plan by which all professional personnel will be evaluated by the results they achieve. If educators go through the time-consuming task of setting objectives with no follow-through, the program is doomed to failure. To prevent this from occurring, top line administrators must be absolutely behind the program and must be willing to open up the communication network so that various staff members have the necessary information in order to set performance objectives and follow through on their attainment.

School MBO is not just another planning procedure; it is also a style or method of managing the operations of the school system which is rewarding and challenging. Before the program is initiated, the superintendent and his central administrative staff must understand what is involved and the problems and difficulties which are likely to occur. When the chief school officer becomes knowledgeable about the School MBO concept, he and the School MBO advisor[1] should personally oversee the program so that it is properly implemented in the school district.

Expect Reasonable First-Year Progress

Remember, Rome was not built in a day! The full value of School MBO will not be realized during the first year of its inception. The program should be viewed as a long-range goal, with aspects of the program being achieved over short-range periods. During the initial stages, the primary interest should be to get educators to think and to act in terms of objectives and to provide time for the concept to develop.

Initially, performance objectives will be written poorly by many staff members. This is to be expected. However, with time, training and experience, this problem should be corrected. Each educator should be given the opportunity to proceed in the program according to his own individual pace and abilities.

Where School MBO is properly implemented, it can be expected that the following changes will be observed:

1. Staff members begin to become result oriented rather than activity oriented.
2. Communication network is improved, resulting in better attitudes about the job itself, improvement in staff morale, sense of purpose for performing, greater respect between educator and his immediate supervisor, etc.
3. Greater proficiency in developing performance objectives and plans.
4. Improvement in individual and overall performance.
5. Motivation for developing constructive innovations.
6. Basis for designing training programs.

---

[1]The position of School MBO advisor is clarified in Chapter 11.

At the end of the first year of the program, some of these items can be expected to occur to varying degrees.

Appoint School MBO Advisor

Although MBO can be implemented in a school district without the assistance of an advisor, the author does not recommend it. It is difficult to implement such a managerial framework or system in a school district and get ultimate results. The various steps in the sequential development of School MBO are precise, time consuming and, to the novice, difficult to achieve. Neither administrators, supervisors, nor teachers are trained properly, for the most part, to implement this approach to operating the school district. Without an advisor, mistakes and misconceptions (particularly the latter) may go unnoticed from review period to review period and year after year with no corrective actions taken. The School MBO advisor is charged with the full responsibility for installing the system and making certain that this approach is implemented smoothly. (Further discussion on the role of the advisor is covered in Chapter 11.) An advisor should be selected and trained in the intricacies of implementing School MBO. The School MBO advisor is a source for professional advice on the entire program. It is his responsibility to develop suitable techniques and methods with the educators, counsel educators in the preparation of the improvement guides and plans, attend review sessions to offer advice, and develop training programs. His role is that of an educator in the true sense of the term and a catalyst for motivating responsive action toward results.

Keep Paper Work to a Minimum

Some administrators who have been involved in the implementation of School MBO have indicated that teachers and administrators have complained about the paper work involved in installing the program. Nothing could be more detrimental to the success of a program than unnecessary administrative details. Paper work and clerical chores required to administer School MBO should be kept to the absolute minimum consistent with effective control. The only reports which should be required for completion are the Individual Improvement Guide, School/Department Improvement Plan and Individual Improvement Plan. All of the necessary information for recording key results analysis, performance objectives, action plans, performance review, should be indicated on these forms. It is unlikely that additional forms will be needed.

Consider a Modest Beginning

At times it is more desirable to implement School MBO in one or two departments or schools rather than throughout an entire school district. In any case, the central administration office should be the first unit or department in the school district to implement the concept. This should help to demonstrate the commitment to the program on the part of the top administrators. This will enable the school administrators to regard this modest beginning as experimental, thereby gaining experience on a limited basis before extending the program. If such is the case, the measuring period should be increased to a six-month period rather than be held to a quarterly basis. The exact length of time should be predicated on the basis of the performance objectives and action plans selected so that there is sufficient time to make progress.

INTRODUCTION PROCEDURES

Develop a Timetable for Installing School MBO

The School MBO advisor should establish a timetable for installing various phases of the concept in the school district. The timetable, which could take the form of a Gantt Chart, will enable the advisor to employ more effective planning before initiating the concept and, most importantly, it provides improved control once the program has been installed.

Essentially the Gantt Chart consists of a series of horizontal open bars, each representing a given amount of planned accomplishment over a projected period of time. Immediately below each bar is a second contrasting solid bar representing actual achievement as of a particular date. At a glance, one is able to determine whether an activity is above plan, on plan, or below plan. The Gantt Chart can be used to chart any activity that has been planned and that requires time to complete. An example of the Gantt Chart approach to installing School MBO is illustrated in Figure 3-2.

Conduct Briefing Session With Administrators

The advisor should schedule briefing sessions in small groups and by departments. After introducing the concept to the group, the advisor describes the system, discusses the policies and procedures for installing School MBO, and answers questions posed by individual members of the group. These brief-

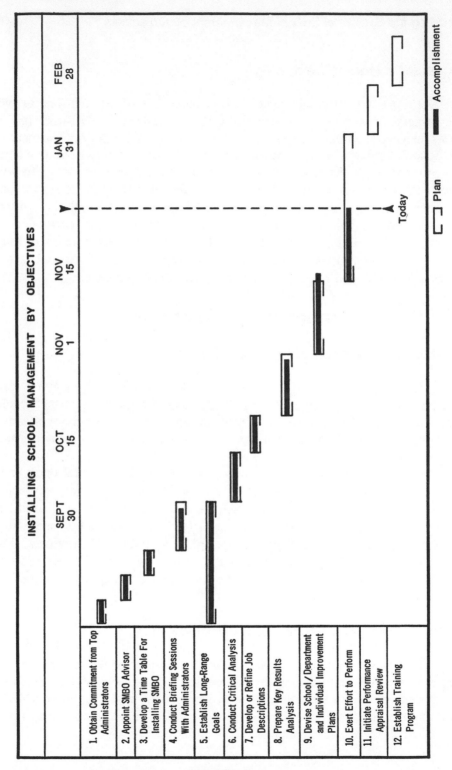

FIGURE 3-2
Gantt Chart for Installing School Management by Objectives

ing sessions provide an opportunity for educators to air their individual doubts and skepticisms about the concept. Some school districts have been known to call in outside consultants to assist the advisor in familiarizing the personnel with School MBO, while other school districts have afforded opportunities for their top administrators to attend workshops and seminars conducted by the American Management Association, University of Michigan and Academy of Administrators' Services. These seminars will provide opportunities for educators to discuss case studies, explore practical problems, and rub shoulders with others who have had experience with the concept. Discussion with the so-called "experts" is also a useful technique for exposing the program to neophytes and for skeptics.

Much can be learned by visiting school systems which have implemented the program. The following schools have implemented MBO:

Baltimore Public Schools Baltimore, Maryland	Westport Public Schools Westport, Connecticut
Trenton Public Schools Trenton, New Jersey	Bloomfield Hills Public Schools Bloomfield Hills, Michigan
Oakland Public Schools Oakland, California	White Plains Public Schools White Plains, New York
Winnetka Public Schools Winnetka, Illinois	Skokie School District 68 Skokie, Illinois

There are a number of films on MBO with accompanying materials which should be of some assistance in briefing school personnel to the intricacies of this concept:

Management by Objectives
   A film for introducing the concept.
Analyzing the Manager's Job
   This film deals with key result analysis and improvement plans.

For further information, the reader may wish to contact BNA Films, Cineconference Center, 5615 Fishers Lane, Rockville, Maryland 20852.

A workbook entitled *Training Guide for Installing Management by Objectives in Education* may be obtained from the following address for the price of $4.50 per copy: T & M Enterprises, Ltd., 731 Franklin Street, Westbury, New York 11590.

IDENTIFYING A STRATEGY FOR INSTALLING SCHOOL MBO

While the author does not maintain that the following strategy is the ideal or only way to actually begin the installation of School MBO, it has been successful in practice and may be of assistance to those school districts that are implementing this concept for the first time:

Step One — Establish Long-Range Goals

The first step in installing School MBO should be for the board of education and the superintendent to mutually agree on some long-range goals for the school district.

One of the major problems of the superintendent in proposing long-range goals to the board of education is getting adequate assistance in formulating them. The prime source for this assistance should come from his staff. A superintendent can always develop long-range goals himself, but in a large school district, this becomes less and less desirable. The following are some suggestions which have been used by some school districts to use staff assistance successfully in developing long-range goals:

1. The chief school officer can initiate a freewheeling "think" session by getting the long-range goal session started. One school superintendent made arrangements for his top school administrators to attend a resort in the mountains, away from the daily routines of the school system, to encourage in-thinking, dialoguing and planning about long-range goals. The summer may be a convenient time to perform long-range goal setting.
2. The superintendent can develop his own draft of long-range goals for the school district and then request each administrator and supervisor to comment and to make suggestions.
3. The chief school officer can ask each administrator and supervisor to draft individual and school or department long-range goals and use these drafts for formulating district-wide long-range goals and priorities.
4. The superintendent can assign School MBO to an advisor with the responsibility for formulating long-range goals for the school district after meeting in either individual or group sessions with administrators and supervisors.
5. The superintendent can meet with his top administrators and supervisors to form a committee to prepare priorities and long-range goals for the school district.

Remember, regardless of the plan used, the district-wide long-range goals which have been formulated are proposals only. It is the responsibility of the board of education and the superintendent to mutually agree to the district-wide long-range goals which are to receive first priority for the school year.

Step Two — Conduct Critical Analysis

When the key results analysis has been completed and mutually agreed to by all parties concerned, the next step involves a critical examination of all available data to determine needs and priorities.

A review of the following data is recommended before proceeding with the construction of improvement plans:

1. Needs Assessment Report (Critical Analysis)
2. Past and present long-range goals and short-range objectives
3. Individual Improvement Guide

Armed with the above data, the administrator, his immediate supervisor, and the School MBO advisor discuss achievement necessary to get the desired results, problems and obstacles which are retarding objective attainment, and what potentials could be maximized to get on- or above-plan performance.

Some of the questions these educators may consider are:

- Should there be a change in the basic design of the organization structure?
- Should the system and reports used to check performance be changed?
- How should the school or department prepare to meet future conditions?
- Should higher performance standards be set?
- What are the most important things the school or department can accomplish this present school year?
- What are the budget limitations?
- Should the school or department establish new approaches for developing staff, improving communication, morale, etc.?
- What are the most important "people" problems facing the school or department and what must be done to solve them?

Step Three — Develop or Refine Job Descriptions

If a job description is not available for every professional position in the school district, then one should be developed. If job descriptions are available for all school positions, they should be scrutinized for completeness, clarity and recency. Then each should be revised, modified and refined so that it can be used as an effective instrument for conducting a job analysis.

The job description " . . . should be constructed to specify each educator's responsibility for the design, maintenance, and efficient operation of a particular production sub-system."[2] Greater emphasis should be on each person's role and responsibility as it pertains to results-oriented tasks than on activities *per se*. The assistant superintendent of instruction controls a production sub-system which is designed to produce the necessary curriculum and instructional materials in order for the school system to fulfill its function in this area. Every educator must realize that he controls a production sub-system by virtue of the fact that he is expected to produce some kind of measurable result.

Step Four — Prepare Key Results Analysis (Individual Improvement Guide)

Each educator must be clear as to the results expected of him in line with established proven policies, procedures, educational and long-range goals, or he may direct his time and energy into trivial tasks. In addition, there will be no agreement upon criteria for appraising performance. Although in most school districts it is assumed that administrators, supervisors and teachers already know what is expected of them, in fact many are quite unclear as to what is expected of them.

Shortly after the critical analysis has been conducted, key results required from each administrator and supervisor are analyzed. The key results analysis is usually recorded on a form known as the Individual Improvement Guide. It is a useful method for the educator to use in analyzing his key tasks, setting performance standards, suggesting methods for checking and improving performance. Usually a draft of the Guide is discussed with the immediate supervisor and is mutually agreed to by the parties concerned. The Guide also contains the main purpose of the job, the educator's position in the school system, his scope in terms of job responsibility (staff, materials and facilities), key tasks, personal job activity not delegated by the educator, and his limits of authority. A detailed Individual Improvement Guide is illustrated in Chapter 9 and in the Appendix.

---

[2]Human Resource Management, Vol. 11, No. 1, spring, 1972, Bureau of Industrial Relations. The Graduate School of Business Administration, the University of Michigan. Gerard F. Carvalho, "Installing Management by Objectives: A New Perspective on Organization Change," p. 27.

Step Five — Devise School/Department and Individual Improvement Plans

Each administrator and supervisor must make his choice of priority for improvement and consider the resources available. These educators must then construct a School/Department Improvement Plan, citing problems, setting objectives and developing action plans for improving performance. The plan is mutually agreed to by the principal or department head and his immediate supervisor. The School/Department Improvement Plan is then broken down into a series of results expected by various staff members within that school or department and expressed in the form of an Individual Improvement Plan. The Individual Improvement Plan contains the performance objectives, action plans, target dates, persons to initiate the actions, and expected results outcome. Samples of a School/Department Plan and Individual Improvement Plan are indicated in Chapter 10 and in the Appendix.

Step Six — Exert Effort to Perform

Each administrator and supervisor now has his key results analysis (Individual Improvement Guide), school or department plan (School/Department Improvement Plan), and individual plan (Individual Improvement Plan), so that he should be quite clear as to what is expected of him in terms of measurable results. He should now be performing his various tasks to obtain the desired results. At this stage, administrators and supervisors should exercise proper controls so that below-plan performance will be corrected for on- or above-plan performance. The educator should seek advice on problems he cannot solve by himself. His supervisor, during normal discussion with his staff, should be checking on program and results.

Step Seven—Initiate Performance Appraisal Review

The performance appraisal review takes place in two steps. Step One: The educator evaluates his own performance in light of the projected objectives. He records his assessment in the "result outcome" section of his School/Department Plan and/or Individual Improvement Plan. All above- and on-plan performance must be substantiated.

The supervisor reviews his staff member's performance assessment by discussing each objective. In some cases, the supervisor will ask his staff member to substantiate his assessment if it is not in agreement with his own appraisal. The primary intent of Step Two is for both parties to reach a mutual understanding and agreement on results attained. At this time, performance objectives and action plans may be revised, modified, or deleted and new objectives may be defined.

Step Eight—Establish Training Program

A training program should be established by reviewing each educator's performance appraisal review report and listing each area where weaknesses are indicated. In this way, the training course or program is tailored to the unique needs of each individual. The training program is elaborated on in Chapter 12.

AFTER THE INSTALLATION PHASE: REPORTING RESULTS

When School MBO has been fully implemented in the school district and at the first year of operation (and thereafter), all professional staff members should be assembled in a large auditorium to hear a series of reports prepared by the chief school officer, members of the central administration, and each building principal. Each administrator should cover the following:

1. Identify objectives set by departments and the school for the school year.
2. Discuss those objectives achieved on- or above-plan.
3. Explain the reason for those objectives below-plan.
4. Indicate new objectives for the following school year.

Odiorne states that when this type of meeting takes place at the end of the school year, it has a powerful effect on group opinion and influence. He further maintains, "The strong influence which a promise or commitment can have upon subordinates is beneficial in stimulating them to change their directions, their behavior, and their attitudes. At the same time, for the individual who has bad luck, or through no fault of his can't meet his commitments, the possibility of facing a group of peers can be strongly unpleasant."[3] On the other hand, such a meeting will prevent administration from deceiving peers about the performance of their individual department or school. This large group meeting on results of performance is also useful in recognizing the individual and collective achievement of a department or school and certainly is a means of continuing the motivation for improved performance.

---

[3]George S. Odiorne, *Personnel Administration by Objectives*, Richard D. Irwin, Inc., Homewood, Illinois.

The following are some problems associated with the implementation of School MBO and some solutions to these conditions:

Problems	Solution
1. Poorly written performance objectives or objectives written describing activities instead of results.	Establish a training workshop for writing correctly written performance objectives. Develop a procedural guide for writing performance objectives and distribute to the staff. Provide opportunities for educators to progress at their own rate of speed.
2. Setting of low-risk-bearing objectives.	Initially, some educators will develop low-risk-bearing objectives. This is to be expected. The supervisor should be on the alert for these persons. An attempt should be made by the supervisor to persuade them to develop more challenging objectives.
3. Failure to achieve objectives as planned.	There will be instances when an educator will fail to achieve the projected results. These experiences can be useful for guiding the educator for the next objective-setting conference. Obviously, the new objectives should be more in line with reality and attainability.
4. Falsifying statements about the achievement of objectives.	All on- and above-plan performance should be substantiated by either personal observation or documentation. An explanation must follow all below-plan performance.

Problems	Solutions
5. Difficulties in deciding how to initiate the School MBO program.	There are several ways to initiate the School MBO program: a) A long-range plan b) PPBS approach c) Emanating from the central administration down to individual principal and teachers d) Performance appraisal approach e) Key results analysis approach. The program can be implemented using one of the above approaches or combination of same. The author advocates the key result analysis approach emanating from the central administration down to individual principal and teachers.
6. Administrators complaining that they do not have sufficient time to work on the school MBO.	School MBO is a systematic way of operating a school district. It is a method for planning and controlling the activities of the schools so that meaningful effort is exerted in the direction of achieving the philosophy, objectives and goals of the school district. It is the daily responsibility of each educator within the system to plan, set, and achieve objectives for the improvement of the school district.
7. Substantial amount of paper work and time.	If the communication gap is going to be improved through the School MBO program, obviously this is going to entail more of the time of the educators in terms of verbal and written communication. The written communication should consist of a job description, an improvement guide and improvement plans. There is a close association between the amount of communication employed in the program and the success of the program.

Problems	Solutions
8. Lack of commitment to the School MBO program on part of individual administrators.	A lack of commitment to the School MBO program can be attributed to two main reasons: (1) the superintendent or the immediate superintendent has not demonstrated this commitment to the program, and (2) the staff have not been properly trained to implement the School MBO program. By hiring a School MBO advisor to oversee the program, many associated problems will quickly be resolved.
9. Some educators are reluctant to participate in the School MBO for a number of reasons.	The following activities can be used to stimulate interest in the School MBO program: a) Hire a School MBO advisor. b) Circulate School MBO literature and films. c) Provide opportunities for educators to visit school districts which have implemented a School MBO program. d) Use "seed" educators to set examples. Have them discuss particulars about the program with others. e) Establish a real climate for the participatory decision-making policy so that all appropriate personnel are involved in the decision-making process. f) Enhance knowledge and understanding of School MBO program through outside consultants, analysts, School MBO policies, procedures and tasks.
10. Educator is not able to qualify objectives.	Ask educator to describe the results expected in observable terms. Use more than one party to judge the results—e.g., team of experts.

SUMMARY

The preliminary steps for installing School MBO are: (1) to obtain a commitment from the top administrators; (2) to expect reasonable first-year results; (3) to appoint School MBO advisor; (4) to keep paper work to a minimum; (5) to consider a modest beginning. The introductory procedures are: (1) develop a time table for installing the system; (2) conduct briefing sessions with administrators.

A strategy for installing School MBO may consist of eight steps: Step One—establish long-range goals; Step Two—conduct critical analysis; Step Three—develop or refine job descriptions; Step Four—prepare key results analysis; Step Five—devise school department and individual improvement plans; Step Six—exert effort to perform; Step Seven—initiate performance appraisal review; Step Eight—establish training program.

The final stage for installing School MBO for the first year and thereafter is to assemble all the educators in the auditorium and have each administrator report the results of his department or school.

FOUR

Writing the MBO Performance Standards

Standards can be developed for a particular school function as well as for an individual position. For example, conditions can be described which will prevail when the personnel department is doing an adequate job. Standards can also be set which will be indicative of conditions under which the business department can be said to be doing a good job. Standards can also be developed for the entire school system. Such standards would describe the philosophy of the school organization as a whole.

The establishment of performance standards for administrative positions is a relatively recent development, particularly in education. It is possible to set such standards for any position: president of board of education, superintendent of schools, principals, departmental chairmen and teachers. The task is more difficult at lower levels and the method of measurement will probably be more subjective; nevertheless standards for administration and teaching are valid and necessary. The intent of this chapter is to define performance standards, to describe a technique for developing performance standards, to identify examples of performance standards, and to state the advantages of devising performance standards.

DEFINING PERFORMANCE STANDARDS

The writing of performance standards should be handled with extreme care and in all cases should be developed objectively. Objective performance standards should answer these questions: What conditions must prevail? In what manner? How well? Thus the satisfactory performance standards for a business administrator might be expressed as follows:

What conditions must prevail?	Cost accounting must be maintained.
In what manner?	The report must be accurate, up to date, and in conformity with State Education Department's rules and regulations.
How well?	The report must show actual expenditure.

There are an indefinite number of measurable factors that could be used as performance standards. Each educator must make his own determination as to which standards will best serve his purpose:

Staff turnover rate
Promotions
Parent complaints/praises
Relationship established
Ideas generated
Changes initiated
Problems and opportunities spotted
Educational learning packets produced
Academic achievement growth
Number of interviews
Rate of success
Reduction of failures
Attendance
Number of books read
Consensus
Response time
Number of students above grade level
Number of proposals approved for funding

Number of manuscripts produced by staff
Number of school conferences visited
Specific requirements
Number of college graduates returning to the community
Years of experience
Calendar time
Students' days-out rate
Cost reductions
Accident rate
Number of staff members
Degree of acceptance
Materials consumption
Education technology utilization
Percent of proposals passed by board of education
Schedule milestones
Cost for students
Number and nature of reports published
Observation days

DESCRIBING A TECHNIQUE FOR DEVELOPING PERFORMANCE STANDARDS

There are two important steps in stating performance standards so that accurate measures of results are indicated:

1. Begin by thinking about the total job so that all major job divisions of the position can be delineated. List and describe key areas for adequately satisfying the position requirements.
2. Define each major job subdivision by beginning with the words, "Performance will be satisfactory when . . . ." Complete this sentence by specifying the conditions which must prevail to get the required results.

IDENTIFYING EXAMPLES OF PERFORMANCE STANDARDS

Typical areas in which performance standards are developed in the school system for individual administrative, supervisory, and teaching positions include personnel, guidance, research and development, finance, curriculum and instruction. In fact, performance standards should be developed for all administrative, supervisory, and teaching positions in the school system. Some schools have advanced the process by developing performance standards which, when written precisely, are more useful than those which are written elaborately. Performance standards are usually developed to cover duties, responsibilities and relationships with others. All available materials and resources should be referred to in writing performance standards, including past experiences and present operating policies and procedures.

The following excerpts are from the performance standards of administrative and supervisory positions of a small school district located in the northeast section of the country. Each was developed by the individual administrator and supervisor, with his respective supervisor participating. Performance is considered satisfactory when the person's main job subdivisions are being achieved and the stated conditions are being met.

Assistant Superintendent for Personnel:

Main Job Subdivision	Performance Standard
Recruits competent teachers.	A minimum of five years of experience for 75% of new teachers.
Develops an attractive recruitment brochure.	Multiple color with ample pictures is used.
Collaborates with building principals when recruiting.	Teachers recruited do not leave because of unsuitability or job dissatisfaction.

High School Principal:

Main Job Subdivision	Performance Standard
Provides for an interchange of views and ideas by creating a democratic atmosphere.	A minimum of two meetings for each department per year is attended. An "open door" policy for teachers is established to air their views. Monthly staff meetings are conducted.
Evaluates the effectiveness of each staff member.	A minimum of two observations per teacher is conducted per semester, each followed by a conference. A written evaluation form is completed for each teacher, with individual teacher conferences.
Encourages staff toward professional growth.	Staff is alerted concerning all pertinent offerings at the local universities.
Organizes and conducts in-service programs if needed.	A survey is conducted to determine staff needs.

Department Chairman Math/Computer

Main Job Subdivision	Performance Standard
Reviews and updates all courses.	Courses reflect SSMCIS concepts as well as computer applications.
Incorporates computer labs in all courses.	Each course has a supplemental guide of relevant computer applications.
Develops and distributes curriculum guides.	All teachers receive a course curriculum guide.
Keeps abreast with innovations in curriculum.	Current ideas are discussed at department meetings.
Solicits student reaction to course offerings.	Semi-annual student evaluations show enough interest to maintain electives.

Elementary Teacher

Main Job Subdivision	Performance Standard
Communicates the progress of individual students to parents.	Four written reports are issued to parents per school year; Three conferences are held with parents per school year.
Complies with school regulations regarding meetings and reports.	All meetings are attended on time; All reports are submitted one day in advance.
Presents a variety of academic subjects.	The following is adhered to: Reading-------------1½ hr. daily Math-----------------1½ hr. daily Social Science -----1 hr. daily Language Arts -----1 hr. daily Sciences------------3 hrs. weekly Health --------------2 hrs. weekly
Charts student's progress.	Student's profile is maintained in math and reading.

ADVANTAGES OF STATING PERFORMANCE STANDARDS

When performance standards are developed, understood and mutually agreed to by the parties concerned, they offer the following potential benefits, as stated by George L. Morrisey:

1. Yardstick for determining whether or not an objective is going to be achieved.
2. Means for assessing educator's performance.
3. Incentive for performance improvement.
4. Incentive for creative approaches to work performance.
5. Means of self-assessment and correction.
6. Means of interpreting the performance of other educators.
7. Means of projecting future needs.
8. Incentive and means for continuous and consistent re-examination of plans and results.
9. Means of comparing performance of other individuals, departments and schools.[1]

SUMMARY

The development of performance standards should be handled with extreme care and in all cases should be developed objectively. Objective performance standards should answer these questions: What conditions must prevail? In what manner? How well? There are two steps for developing performance standards: (1) list and describe key areas for adequately satisfying the position requirements; (2) define each job subdivision by beginning with the words, "Performance will be satisfactory when . . . ." Complete this sentence by specifying the conditions which must prevail to get the required results.

Typical areas in which performance standards are developed in the school system include individual, administrative, supervisory and teaching positions. Performance objectives refer to a desired improvement in results. Performance standards are the conditions that will exist when results in key areas are satisfactory.

---

[1]George L. Morrisey, *Management by Objectives and Results*, Addison Wesley, Reading, Mass., 1970, p. 110.

FIVE

Monitoring Performance for Improved Results

Monitoring performance in a school district is regarded as one of the most difficult tasks confronting administrators and supervisors. This may account for the fact that so few supervising educators establish the procedures for effective and consistent monitoring of performance. The purpose of monitoring performance is to provide the school district with the necessary information to make decisions regarding corrective action to achieve objectives. Monitoring methods and techniques for checking performance are used to regulate the school organization in order to maintain a condition which is dynamic and sensitive to change for obtaining the desired results. This chapter will identify the purpose for monitoring performance, explain the cycle, identify the essential ingredients for monitoring performance, discuss the *what, how,* and *when to* of monitoring performance, provide some examples and discuss basic assumptions about monitoring performance.

IDENTIFYING THE PURPOSE FOR MONITORING PERFORMANCE

The administrator or supervisor who wishes to manage his school or department successfully must be able to recognize and understand the dynamic nature of the components of the school district. In a home, the thermostat is used to adjust for the variations in the physical environment; in the school, the administrator and/or supervisor must sense and respond to changes within an individual school or department. Monitoring performance is the function whereby administrators and supervisors identify changes which will affect attainment of objectives, discuss reasons for making changes and make the necessary adjustments in order to achieve the desired results. In brief, the purpose of monitoring performance is to provide the school district with effective management information, guides to decision-making, and bases for taking corrective action in order to ensure that the projected objectives will be attained. Monitoring performance is the final step for an administrator or supervisor, after he has planned properly, structured programs, staffed adequately, and delegated wisely for the effective operation of the school district.

BASIC ASSUMPTIONS ABOUT MONITORING PERFORMANCE

The impetus for designing and using various methods for monitoring performance comes from a recognition on the part of administrators and supervisors that:

- Maximum effort has not been exerted on the part of educators to improve performance; therefore performance must be monitored.
- Planning without proper follow-through does not get the desired results.
- Once time has elapsed and efforts have been extended it is usually too late or costly to take corrective action.
- Each educator needs adequate methods and procedures for checking the· progress of objectives.
- Administrators and supervisors must have adequate methods for checking all activities that contribute to attainment of objectives.
- Educational accountability can be implemented effectively only if there is a method for checking performance and taking the necessary corrective actions.

MONITORING PERFORMANCE CYCLE

One of the most widely accepted and used approaches to monitoring performance in business and industry, which can be easily adapted to education, is the closed-loop model shown in Figure 5-1. It can be seen from the model that first the educator must set the objective, develop performance standards, and lay out an action plan for achieving the objective. The cycle is completed when the objective is achieved as projected. Between the time the objective is set and achieved, monitoring performance is set in motion for the administrators and supervisors to perform certain administrative or supervisory functions. The proper monitoring of performance requires that standards of performance and the action plan be developed which will directly affect the attainment of the objective. The net result of the effort that has been exerted to perform is then evaluated to determine whether or not performance has been above-, on-, or below-plan. If performance is below-plan, the necessary corrective action is initiated to achieve the objective. The reader can readily understand that each phase of the cycle is important; if one element is overlooked, the process of monitoring performance adequately will be impaired.

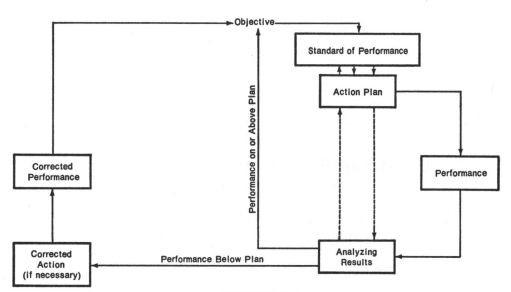

FIGURE 5-1
Closed-Loop Model for Monitoring Performance

IDENTIFYING THE ESSENTIAL INGREDIENTS FOR MONITORING PERFORMANCE

The success or failure of the School MBO program rests with how well the system of monitoring performance has been adapted and implemented in the school district. To increase the probability of success of the program, the process for monitoring performance should contain the following ingredients:

1. A basic understanding of performance objective so that every educator knows the purpose for monitoring performance and what is required of him.

2. There should be joint participation by the educator and his immediate supervisor in the development of methods for checking performance.

3. Satisfactory performance should be identified in terms of performance objectives, standards of performance and action plans so that these combined elements constitute minimum acceptability.

4. Performance should be closely supervised so that action can be exerted where performance is below plan.

5. The immediate supervisor should conduct periodic on-the-job inspection to determine if the result expected will be met.

6. Self-assessment should be built into the system so that self-correction of below-planned performance can be made.

7. Whenever possible, methods for checking performance should be physically observed.

8. Below-plan performance should be reported to immediate supervisor as soon as possible.

9. Methods for monitoring performance should be consistent with school objectives, policies and procedures.

10. Methods should be developed which allow adaptation to individual situations and changes in the school or department environment.

UNDERSTANDING THE WHAT, HOW, AND WHEN TO MONITOR PERFORMANCE

Developing a method for monitoring performance requires answers to three basic questions by administrators and supervisors:

What to Monitor

The decision regarding what must be monitored in terms of performance must be based on the recognition of critical areas, trouble spots, ineffective personnel, and what must be evaluated against the objective or action plan.

How to Monitor

The decision regarding how to monitor is concerned with the method or technique for checking performance. Obviously the method should not be too costly or too time consuming. The best methods or techniques for monitoring performance are those activities that will indicate current status quickly with a minimum amount of demand from the administrators or superiors.

When to Monitor

The decision regarding when to monitor is concerned primarily with the time in which progress is to be evaluated and the extent of the action necessary to correct for below-plan performance. The following are some sample illustrations for monitoring performance:

High School Principal

Performance Standard	Method of Checking Performance
A balanced staff is maintained as follows: a. 50% over 10 years' experience. b. 15% minority members.	Administrative assistant will verify ratio; employment application.
Lists are provided by administrative assistant indicating certified substitutes only.	Payroll dept. maintains checklist of all certified staff members and substitutes.
Two student teachers are assigned to departments each spring semester: one to math and one to English departments.	Report of compliance submitted to assistant superintendent for the institutional program by June 1st of each year by math and English department chairmen.
The school has 8 periods of 45 minutes each. Each teacher has 5 duty assignments: a. One preparation period b. One lunch period c. Three professional periods for meetings, conferences and remedial work with students.	Assistant principal submits duty assignment on all teachers to principal by second week of school in September.
Teachers have three preparations at most. At least 50% of teachers have two preparations.	Department chairman to submit final schedule assignments to principal on second day of each school term.
The following is maintained: a. Pupil accounting records of daily attendance. b. Permanent record cards. c. Cumulative guidance folders.	Maintain: a. Responsibility of attendance officer who must submit daily attendance report to principal by 11 o'clock. b. Responsibility of guidance department chairman who must update and maintain permanent record cards on all students by Oct. 1 and March 1 of each year. c. (Same as item b.)

High School Principal (continued)

Performance Standard	Method of Checking Performance
d. Follow-up report on all graduates commencing with class of '70.	d. Responsibilities of director of pupil personnel who must submit annual report to principal and superintendent by Dec. 1 of each year.

Chairman of English Department

Performance Standard	Method of Checking Performance
The cost for department kept within the projected $8,000.00. Teacher requisitions are turned in to chairman by Dec. 15 of each school year.	Monthly financial statement from principal; department's cost accounting records. Log book.
Performance objectives are written and mutually agreed upon. 100% of students are tested in reading and language arts skills by Sept. 15 of school year.	Verbal/written conferences; staff and department performance review reports. Charts, norms; diagnostic reports on individual students by Oct. 15 of school year.

Monitoring performance is essential for the growth and development of the total school organization. Through this process, self-assessing, self-supervising and self-correcting produce self-directed school personnel for improved performance.

SUMMARY

The purpose of monitoring performance is to provide the school district with effective information, decisive rules, and the means to take corrective action in such a manner as to achieve objectives. One of the most widely accepted and used approaches to monitoring performance in business and industry which can be applied to education is the closed-loop model. This model begins with the educators setting the objective, establishing standards of performance, and laying out an action plan for achieving the objective.

The success or failure of the School MBO program rests largely with how well the system of monitoring performance has been adopted and implemented in the school district. *What to monitor* refers to critical areas, trouble spots, ineffective personnel, and what must be evaluated against the objective and action plan. *How to monitor* refers to the method or technique designed to check performance. *When to monitor* refers to the time element.

SIX

Setting Goals and Objectives

Although there are many facets to producing the most desirable working climate in a school district, clearly specified performance objectives are a first and essential requirement for developing and maintaining a high level of job satisfaction and motivation among the professional staff members. Without definite goals and objectives to which school personnel will direct their individual effort, a sense of purpose and accomplishment will be noticeably absent and effort will tend to be directed toward maintaining the status quo. Furthermore, without clearly defined goals and objectives the educator may find himself constantly on the defensive due to the fact that there has been no previous agreement on desired results. He may be criticized because he has not maintained the results his immediate supervisor thought he would attain; obviously this is unfair to the educator and no doubt will debilitate his morale. This chapter will define long-range goals and short-range objectives, identify the various kinds of performance objectives, state essential ingredients of performance objectives, point up the advantages of stating long-range goals and short-range objectives, declare "do's" and "don'ts" for setting objectives, demonstrate the relationship between long-range goals and short-range objectives, and suggest ways to follow up on setting objectives.

DEFINING LONG-RANGE GOALS

Long-range goals are broad task assignments or end results for an individual or group to achieve over a period of three years or more, and are

75

therefore specific and measurable. These are goals in line with the school district's philosophy and educational objectives. A classic definition of a goal is stated by Charles L. Hughes:

> A goal is an end, a result, not just a task or function to be performed. It is a place in space and time that describes the condition we want to achieve. It is a standard of achievement, a criterion.of success, something tangible, measurable, and vulnerable that we are motivated toward. It is concrete and explicit, definitive and desirable and predetermined. It guides our actions and helps us plan as teachers and administrators. It can be long range or short range; long-range goals help clarify our short-range goals, major goals determine minor goals, and the present is determined by the future —not the past.[1]

Each long-range goal should begin with "to increase, to provide, to develop," etc. Also, each long-range goal should state, "from _____" and "to_____" and "over __*[period]*__." Two examples of long-range goals are as follows:

> To convert from the line budget to program planning and budgeting system by June 30, 19__ (3 years).
> To increase the percentage of primary students reading on grade level from 35% to 90% by June, 19__ (3 years).

Long-range goals are sometimes stated with one or more constraints:

Standards: (constraints)

1. As measured by the Metropolitan Achievement Test, which is to be administered by an outside agency.
2. Annual test results to be distributed to the community on an annual basis, no more than three weeks after school terminates for the summer.

Goals are often developed after needs have been determined to correct a deficiency or weakness such as the following:

Needs Assessment:

> *Strength:*
> Professional staff willingness to meet with parents to discuss progress of their children.

---

[1]Charles L. Hughes, "Goal Setting," American Management Association, Inc., New York, N.Y., 1965, p. 8. The author has substituted the word "teachers" for "individuals" and "administrators" for "managers" in the original text of Charles L. Hughes.

Weakness:

Lack of interest and apathy shown on the part of parents by their non-attendance at meetings and letter response.

Long-Range Goal:

To raise the percentage of parental attendance at school meetings from 10% to 60% by June 19___ (3 years).

DEFINING SHORT-RANGE OBJECTIVES

A performance objective is a statement of a personal commitment to perform a specific act that is oriented towards the philosophy of the school district, valuable for achieving its purpose, worthwhile for improving and monitoring performance and time-phased usually within a period of one year (short range) to achieve results.

Short-range objectives should contain the following:

1. Action verb preceded by the word "to."
2. Specific and measurable act.
3. Target date.
4. Criteria for determining successful performance.

The following are examples of well-written performance objectives:

To decrease student absentee rate in school from 20% to 5% by June 15, 19___.

To increase the percentage of competent junior high school mathematics substitute teachers as judged on standardized district-wide evaluation reports from 23% to 75% by June 30, 19___.

Sometimes the citation of a problem is written to illustrate the reason for setting the objective, such as the following:

Problem (What's wrong)	Improvement Action (Objective)
Curriculum orientation must be modernized from subject center to individual skill center to meet the unique needs of each student.	To complete 75 team-teaching, individualized units in the area of English, tenth grade, by June 10, 19___.

Important: The citation of the problem should depict or imply the problematic condition and what should result when it is corrected in line with the projected plan (objective).

IDENTIFYING THE VARIOUS KINDS OF PERFORMANCE OBJECTIVES

The following are the definitions and examples of the various kinds of performance objectives:

Professional skill objectives are clearly defined statements describing critical aspects of typical administrative or teaching performance:

"To visit the classrooms of several exemplary teachers to observe their teaching styles and methods of maintaining classroom control."

"To improve my classroom questioning technique by:
   a. Asking the question first, then calling on the student to answer.
   b. Using the student's response to a question as a springboard for generating interaction among the rest of the class.
   c. Using a maximum of two sentences to elicit responses from the student."

Program objectives are the bases for programs, projects, etc., which are developed and implemented to reach long-range goals.[2]

"To implement continuous progress program in all primary schools."
"To install School Management by Objectives."

Managing objectives are directed toward causing to happen the managing that is necessary to accomplish long-range goals.

"To reorganize the entire school for differentiated staffing."
"To develop a plan for training all assistant principals to implement nongraded education in their respective schools."

Personal development objectives are those of the individual which are directed toward the satisfaction of some of his needs or other personal attainment.

"To attend Teachers College, Columbia University, during the fall semester, 19___, and work toward the completion of the requirements for the Ed.D. degree."
"To complete a minimum of five individual study units which will be tried in a class."

---

[2]Program objectives are sometimes referred to as innovative objectives.

Resource objectives are directed toward providing, developing, and improving resources (personnel, money, machines, materials, space, time, etc.) needed for the accomplishment of long-range goals.

> "To train all K-3 teachers in the school district for implementing the Cureton Reading Program."
>
> "To develop a process for facilitating the implementation of the performance review program."

Problem-solving objectives are emergency objectives which usually evolve when professional skill objectives are not being met.

Problem:

> The school district has a budget deficit of $468,047.00 which must be reduced to zero by June 30, 19___ (4 years).

Objective:

> To prepare and supervise a budget reduction program to reduce this amount from $468,047.00 to $368,047.00 by June 30, 19___ (1 year).

ESSENTIAL INGREDIENTS OF PERFORMANCE OBJECTIVES

Objectives should be:

1. Based upon the objectives of the organizational unit of the educator plus his personal goals.
2. Necessary, and contribute to long-range goals.
   a. They should answer the question, "What vital part of the long-range goal will achieving this objective fulfill?"
   b. They should be ultimately traceable to the organization's educational objectives.
3. Measurable as much as possible in terms of a specific unit or, at least, in terms of trends or degrees of accomplishment.
4. Realistic and attainable; reasonable yet challenging.
5. Relatively few in number; significant and primarily concerned with what must be accomplished.

IDENTIFYING THE RELATIONSHIP BETWEEN LONG-RANGE GOAL AND SHORT-RANGE OBJECTIVE

The relationship between long-range goal and short-range objective, the latter being controlled by periodic review of performance, is illustrated in

LONG-RANGE GOAL (3 YEAR PERIOD)

School Year	1971 – 72	1972 – 73	1973 – 74
1st Quarter Review	Short-Range Objective Developed	Short-Range Objective Modified	
2nd Quarter Review	Short-Range Objective Modified		
3rd Quarter Review	Short-Range Objective Continued as is		
4th Quarter Review	Short-Range Objective Achieved Above Plan		

SHORT–

RANGE

OBJECTIVE

(1 Year Period)

FIGURE 6-1
The Relationship Between Long-Range Goal and Short-Range Objective

Figure 6-1. The long-range goal illustrated is for a three-year period. However, any period of time beyond three years could have been selected. The relationship between long-range goal and short-range objective for the first year of the three-year plan is explained as follows:

The Needs Assessment Report revealed the following—

Teacher Absenteeism

Strength: Some teachers are never absent from school.
Weakness: Many teachers are reported absent from school due to illness, necessitating a budgetary expenditure approximating $60,000.00 each school year.
Need: To reduce the average absentee rate of teachers.

After a discussion by the board of education and superintendent concerning the weakness stated in the Needs Assessment Report, a decision is reached jointly that reducing teacher absentee rate would be one of the priority long-range goals for the school year 19___ .

The chief school officer developed the following long-range goal which was mutually agreed to by the board of education without change:

Long-range goal

To reduce the average absentee rate of teachers from 10 days to 5 days per school year by June 30, 19___ (3 years).

Each building principal was issued a written copy of long-range goals which would be included in their School/Department Improvement Plan.

A review of one of the building principal's School/Department Improvement Plans revealed the following short-range objective:

Improvement Action (Objective)	Step-by-Step Breakdown of Action Required	Target Date
To reduce the average teacher's absentee rate from 10 days to 8. 5 days by June 15, 19___	1. At initial meeting with teachers, stress importance of good attendance.	1. Sept. 8, 19___ .
	2. Post chart displaying teachers' absences in principal's office.	2. Sept. 10, 19___ .
	3. Request meeting with all teachers after fifth absence.	3. As warranted.
	4. Forward congratulatory letter to all teachers who have not been absent for two quarters.	4. As warranted.
	5. Report attendance progress with staff.	5. Two days after each quarter.

The following is an account of the results for the above objective and action plan:

- The first periodic review report on the short-range objective revealed that the objective would be achieved as planned.

- The second periodic review report on this short-range objective indicated that the average absentee rate of teachers for the period is 4.5, well below plan. The principal met with his department chairmen and they mutually agreed to modify Step Three of the action plan as follows:

3— Request meeting with all teachers after *each* absence.

They further agreed that the following activities be included in the action required:

6— Each teacher accumulating six or more absences during a school year will be required to meet with the assistant superintendent for personnel to explain the reason.

- The third periodic review report on the short-range objective revealed that the objective was expected to be achieved on plan.
- The fourth and final periodic review of performance for the first year short-range objective indicated that the average absentee rate for teachers was 7.9, above plan for that particular school. This information was submitted to the central administration office.

In August, 19___, the principal modified his School/Department Improvement Plan in this area as follows:

To reduce the average teacher's absentee rate from 7.9 days to 6 days by June 15, 19___.

This revised version of the first year short-range objective becomes the short-range objective for the second year of the three-year plan.

SUMMARY

Long-range goals are broad task assignments or end results for an individual or group to be achieved over a period of three years or more, and therefore specific and measurable. A performance objective is a statement of a personal commitment to perform a specific act that is oriented towards the philosophy of the school district. Professional skill objectives are clearly defined statements describing critical aspects of typical administrative or teaching performance. Program objectives are the bases for programs, projects, etc., which are developed and implemented to reach long-range goals. Managing objectives are directed toward causing to happen the managing that is necessary to accomplish long-range goals. Personal development objectives are those of the individual which are directed toward the satisfaction of some of his needs or other personal attainment. Resource objectives are directed toward providing, developing, and improving resources needed for the accomplishment of long-range goals. Problem-solving objectives are emergency objectives which usually evolve when professional skill objectives are not being met. Objectives should be: (1) based upon organizational and personal goals; (2) necessary and should contribute to long-range goals; (3) measurable; (4) realistic and attainable; (5) relatively few in number.

SEVEN

Establishing a Plan of Action for Achieving Objectives

Once the performance standards have been stated and the objective has been set, an action plan for reaching the objective must be established. By way of analogy, consider a family that has decided to take a vacation trip. Having decided to go to Florida (terminal goal) for their vacation, the family must now determine "how" it will reach the vacation destination. Some of the avenues (alternatives) they will probably consider are: Should we go by automobile? By plane? By boat? If we go by automobile, what route should we take? Can our automobile get us to our destination without much difficulty?, etc. To some of our readers, establishing an action plan may sound simple. In fact, the actual procedures for laying out an action plan are relatively easy. However, the degree of difficulty will depend to a large extent on the complexity of the objective. The intent of this chapter is to define an action plan, to identify factors affecting the construction of an action plan, to delineate the procedural steps for arriving at an action plan, to demonstrate some objectives and action plans and to identify the advantages of establishing an action plan.

DEFINING AN ACTION PLAN

An action plan is the process of breaking down an objective into sequential steps for its effective accomplishment. It is, in effect, laying out the "route" an administrator or teacher is going to follow in order to achieve an objective. This procedure allows the educator to assess the various methods to be taken to progress toward the objective prior to the initiated action. It will not guarantee that the best means or steps will be selected; it will however, increase greatly the chances of objective attainment provided that all of the alternatives were considered and the best alternative was used as the basis for the action plan. An important value of an action plan is that it may enable the educator to determine if the original estimate of the actions to be taken will, in effect, accomplish the objective. If the actions will not result in the accomplishment of the objective, then the educator must reconsider the objective and/or the plan of action before committing resources and efforts. A well-designed action plan can aid the administrator or teacher in making the most appropriate use of resources. It also provides the kind of visibility necessary to monitor performances to ensure that the objective will be achieved.

FACTORS AFFECTING THE CONSTRUCTION
OF AN ACTION PLAN

The various approaches to constructing an action plan are virtually limitless. The most appropriate approach at a given time is dependent upon many factors, some of which are: the nature of the objectives; the availability of resources; the criticality of scheduling; and the ingenuity and experience of the educator preparing the plan of action. The following are some action plan developmental approaches that have been used by educators in several school districts which have implemented School MBO:

1. *Sequential Organization* — There are certain educational activities which automatically fall in line sequentially. This normally occurs when each step is dependent on the sucessful completion of the preceding step.
2. *Similar Effort* — Two or several steps that require the same type of effort, such as attendance at various conferences for the purpose of acquiring information in order to implement an innovation, can be grouped together.
3. *Terminal Events or Situations* — An action plan sometimes must relate to specific terminal events or situations connected with other objectives. This is particularly true when forming a personal development objective to train or prepare teachers to implement a creative program through an innovative objective.
4. *Technical Development* — Research and development efforts, such as constructing a curriculum guide to implement an innovative program, may have to be made to achieve the objective.
5. *End Event* — Some objectives may relate to specific end events related to other objectives. Example: The completion of a training program which would be the prerequisite to the implementation of the innovation.

6. *Individual or Agency Oriented* — An action plan must sometimes relate to the potential or capability of an individual or agency which must be developed out of sequence in order to fit the timetable of the person or agency.
7. *Political Consideration* — The existence of political influences may have to be considered when developing an action plan for a particular objective.
8. *Cost Consideration* – Cost might be a factor which must be considered when developing an action plan for the attainment of an objective.

PROCEDURAL STEPS FOR CONSTRUCTING AN ACTION PLAN FOR ACHIEVING AN OBJECTIVE

There are eight important steps in constructing a plan of action for achieving an objective. However, some of these steps may not apply to all objectives. In some cases, two or more steps may be combined into a single activity. At times, the specific sequential phase of the action plan may vary and some steps may even be repeated more than once. However, in any event, an action plan can be constructed by using a version of the following eight steps:

1. Study alternatives and select the best one. This step may involve the brainstorming of alternative solutions to the situation or problem and making a decision as to the best alternative, or it may simply involve a view of the situation or problem and a decision as to what measure should be taken to reach the objective.
2. Gain commitment from individuals and/or agencies. This step involves conferring with and gaining commitments from administrators, supervisors, teachers, organizations or any others whose support is necessary for achieving the objective. This step may be extremely important or of little importance, depending on the objective and the degree of support necessary for objective attainment.
3. Develop a plan of action. This step involves the actual layout of a plan of action to be followed for reaching the objectives. There are some essential factors which should be considered when laying out the activities of the action plan. The activities should be:
   a. constructed using an action verb whenever possible, such as "develop."
   b. realistic and attainable.
   c. specific as to what exactly is to be accomplished.
   d. descriptive, leading to achievement of objective.
   e. written using observable terms.
   f. clear as to specific target dates for completion.

4. Project a timetable. A timetable (target date) should be projected for each activity of the action plan. This step is extremely important because without a timetable, the activity or objective may never be achieved.
5. Designate the person and/or activity to be initiated. In the School and Department Improvement Plan the name of the party and the action to be initiated is indicated. In the Individual Improvement Plan only the name of the party to perform the action is indicated.
6. Test and review plan. This step could possibly include a trial run of the plan to determine if the objective is likely to be achieved or it could simply involve a close scrutiny of individual activities so that a determination can be made as to whether or not the objective will be reached.
7. Implement the plan. This step may involve merely the terminal activity of the plan of action or it may be the most significant activity in the plan to achieve the objective.
8. Follow up. This step involves establishing a complete monitoring system or a "check point" system to keep track of the progress of the objective. The successful attainment of the objective will depend to a large extent on how well this step has been incorporated into the activities of the action plan.[1]

IMPORTANT CONSIDERATIONS

The process of developing an action plan for reaching an objective must be approached in a systematic manner by carefully examining the scope and sequence of each step. Failure to do so could result in waste of resources, manpower and money. The following questions should be examined in order to develop an action plan that will succeed in accomplishing the objective:

1. *What vital steps are necessary in order to achieve the objective?*

   The term *vital* refers to major or significant efforts necessary to accomplish the objective. A major activity of an action plan could conceivably be the accomplishment of an objective by another educator: "Assist the director of curriculum and instruction in compiling and editing the fourth grade curriculum guide . . ." could be a vital activity of the plan of action that if not achieved could seriously prevent the successful attainment of the objective.

2. *What priorities should be assigned to each step of the action plan?*

   In every action plan, some steps are more important than others. These "more important" steps must be given priority over the less

---

[1]George C. Morrissey, *Management by Objectives and Results*, Addison-Wesley Publishing Co., Reading, Mass., 1970, pp. 71-72.

important. As an example, training of personnel in a particular program should receive priority over the implementation of the program. Obviously, if the personnel are not trained to implement a certain program, it cannot be implemented successfully. Priorities must also be given to scheduling factors; this is a prime reason why the activities of an action plan must be sequentially structured.

3. *What minor sub-activities are necessary to support major activities for accomplishing an objective?*

    When the overall objective has been formulated, the major activities for achieving the objective must be broken down into minor or sub-activities so that the first activities for attaining the objective are identified and clarified.

4. *What method(s) or mean(s) should be employed to monitor the performance of person(s) or agency(ies) who have a share in the responsibility for accomplishing the objective?*

    Objectives cannot be achieved by mere chance. Some method(s) or means must be initiated so that progress is checked periodically toward objective attainment.

    "To (principal) submit to the reading supervisor, the results of the monthly reading test which is administered to the fourth, fifth and sixth grades . . ." is an example of a method for monitoring the reading results of a school on a monthly basis.

SAMPLE PERFORMANCE OBJECTIVES WITH ACTION PLANS

The following are some examples of performance objectives where action plans were developed. The reader should understand that action plans are formulated to identify those activities and efforts required to achieve the objectives.

Performance Objective and Action Plan for School Improvement Plan

Improvement Action (Objective)	Step-by-Step Breakdown Action Required	Target Date	Action by Administrator
To install a "modular" schedule in the high school by June 30, 19__.	1. Establish a Modular Schedule Committee with representation from each area of instruction.	Oct. 15, 19__.	Asst. principal

Performance Objective and Action Plan for School Improvement Plan (cont.)

Improvement Action (Objective)	Step-by-Step Breakdown Action Required	Target Date	Action by Administrator
	2. Allow committee time to investigate all facets of modular scheduling for a period of two months.	Dec. 15, 19__.	Asst. principal
	3. Consult throughout building to permit open discussion by administration and staff.	Jan. 21, 19__.	Principal
	4. If given "go ahead" by faculty and administration, have master schedule drawn up for school year 19__.	May 1, 19__.	Asst. principal

Performance Objective and Action Plan for Individual Improvement Plan.*

Improvement Action (Objective)	Step-by-Step Breakdown Action Required	Target Date	By Whom
To establish a school professional library of at least 500 works in the room adjoining the main library before June 30, 19__.	1. Request the aid of district director of libraries in creating preliminary budget.	July 26, 19__.	Librarian
	2. Submit budget for approval.	Aug. 15, 19__.	Librarian
	3. At orientation day, explain objective to staff and elicit their support.	Sept.7, 19__.	Librarian
	4. Assign school librarian the responsibility of setting up and maintaining professional library.	Sept. 7, 19__.	Librarian

*The result of this objective and action plan was achieved above plan. The school professional library was established by April 1, 19__, three months ahead of the projected date.

Performance Objective and Action Plan for Individual Improvement Plan. (cont.)

Improvement Action (Objective)	Step-by-Step Breakdown Action Required	Target Date	Action by Administrator
	5. Increase library's secretarial staff from 3 to 5 for 2-month period.	Sept. 15, 19___.	Principal and Asst. Superintendent of Personnel
	6. Assign one teacher aide to full-time duty in main library.	Sept.15, 19___.	Principal
	7. Design physical facilities.	Oct. 1, 19___.	Principal, district director of libraries, librarian, and superintendent of buildings and grounds
	8. Carry out designs.	Dec. 23, 19___.	Building superintendent
	9. Ask faculty for donations of materials.	Dec. 1 19___.	Librarian
	10. Collect lists of works that should be included in library from dept. chairmen.	Dec. 15, 19___.	Librarian
	11. Write letters to community organizations & governmental agencies requesting donations of material & money.	Dec. 1, 19___.	Librarian
	12. Coordinate lists & write purchase orders.	Jan.15, 19___.	Librarian and library typist
	13. Arrange and catalogue additions.	When necessary	Library typist
	14. Publish list of additions in staff bulletin.	Weekly	Librarian
	15. Request individuals of staff to submit reviews of specific works to be distributed to faculty.	Periodically	Principal
	16. Submit Professional Library Budget for 19___.	Apr. 1, 19___.	Librarian

Performance Objective and Action Plan for Department Improvement Plan

Improvement Action (Objective)	Step-by-Step Breakdown Action Required	Target Date	Action by Administrator
To develop and update programs and activities geared to increase student incentive and participation in the math/computer activities by Nov. 1, 19___.	1. Form a computer squad of 4 or 5 students to aid teachers during class and to teach a class in things related to the computer (upon teacher's request).	Sept. 4, 19___.	Math chairman
	2. Give recognition to these students by publicizing their activities.	Nov. 1, 19___.	Math chairman
	3. Enlist honor students to help, during class, tutor students in need.	Nov. 30, 19___.	Math chairman
	4. Have "mathlete" sessions once a week after school & post "problem of the week" examples with a reward going to best solution.	Jan. 1, 19___.	Teachers of honor
	5. Post dates and rewards pertaining to math & science fairs and have teachers encourage participation.	Feb. 1, 19___.	Math teachers
	6. Update curriculum and teaching techniques.	July 1, 19___.	Math chairman
	7. Distribute updated materials to all teachers.	Sept. 5, 19___.	Math chairman
	8. In modified classes have teachers make use of pre-programmed individualized tutor drills in order to individualize the instruction, drill basics, and gain experience with computer hardware.	Sept. 20, 19___.	Math chairman

Performance Objective and Action Plan for Department Improvement Plan (cont.)

Improvement Action (Objective)	Step-by-Step Breakdown Action Required	Target Date	Action by Administrator
	9. In the modified classes exchange, interchange teachers and students who have been scheduled in the same time mod, using the progress of the students on tests given that month as a determination.	Sept. 30, 19___.	All teachers
	10. Enlist the services of tutors from the honor society and student-teachers to help individuals in the modified classes during class.	Nov. 1, 19___.	Math chairman
	11. Set up a computer squad of interested students who will assist teachers with their classes when working in the computer lab on drill exercises, running labs, etc.	Nov.1, 19___.	Math chairman
	12. Set up lab demonstrations for classes that request it.	Nov. 1, 19___.	Math chairman
	13. Prepare tapes that review basic steps used in preparing a lab to be run and the procedure for running it.	Jan. 1, 19___.	Mr. P. Papus & Miss T. Rears
	14. Enlist teachers to spend two weeks during the summer rewriting computer curriculum guides for each senior high school course.	June 12, 19___.	Math chairman

Performance Objective and Action Plan for Department Improvement Plan (cont.)

Improvement Action (Objective)	Step-by-Step Breakdown Action Required	Target Date	Action by Administrator
	15. Enlist 2 teachers to take NSF courses during the summer in SSMCIS Columbia math.	June 12, 19___.	Math chairman

IDENTIFYING THE ADVANTAGES OF ESTABLISHING AN ACTION PLAN

The advantages of developing an action plan for achieving an objective are as follows:

1. It provides a basis for determining the feasibility for achieving the objective.
2. It provides a sound basis for estimating time and resources to accomplish the objective.
3. It helps to determine the most appropriate method for achieving the objective.
4. It helps to identify persons who are to be relied on for support.
5. It helps to establish a procedure for control when the objective and action plan are mutually agreed to by the parties involved.
6. It provides a basis for determining activities which hinder the achievement of the objective.

SUMMARY

An action plan is the process of breaking down an objective into sequential steps for its effective accomplishment. The various approaches to constructing an action plan are virtually limitless. The most appropriate approach at a given time is dependent upon many factors such as the nature of the objective, the availability of resources, the criticality of scheduling and the ingenuity and experience of the person preparing the action plan. Some factors affecting the developing of an action plan are: sequential organization, similar effort, terminal events or situations, technical development, end event, individual or agency oriented, political consideration and cost consideration.

The procedural steps for constructing an action plan for an objective are: (1) Study alternatives and select best one; (2) Gain commitment from individuals and/or agencies; (3) Develop plan of action; (4) Project a timetable; (5) Designate the person and/or activity to be initiated; (6) Test and review plan; (7) Implement the plan; (8) Follow up.

The following questions should be examined in order to develop an action plan that will succeed in accomplishing an objective: (1) What vital steps are necessary in order to achieve the objective? (2) What priorities should be assigned to each step of the action plan? (3) What minor sub-activities are necessary to support major activities for accomplishing an objective? (4) What method (s) or mean (s) should be employed to monitor the performance of person (s) or agency (ies) who have a share in the responsibility for accomplishing the objective?

There are several advantages for establishing an action plan: (1) Used as a basis for determining the feasibility for achieving the objective; (2) Used as a basis for estimating time and resources; (3) Helps to determine most appropriate method for achieving an objective; (4) Helps to identify support reasons; (5) Helps to establish control procedures; (6) Helps to identify activities which may hinder the achievement of objectives.

EIGHT

Conducting the Performance Appraisal Review

The role of the administrator during the performance appraisal review is that of coach and counselor. He assists in identifying problems and hindrances to achieving objectives, and he aids in arriving at solutions to problems. This, to a large extent, is in direct contrast to the traditional form of "evaluation" characterized by an administration-prepared evaluation report which is purely subjective of the educator's performance. The prime objective of the contemporary performance appraisal review is to improve the communication network by establishing two-way communication, remove obstacles to successful achievement of objectives, revise or modify plans if warranted, add new objectives or delete objectives depending upon the situation, and provide an opportunity for coaching and counseling the staff member, thereby improving his performance and the administrator's own effectiveness. This chapter will define a performance appraisal review, identify the basic philosophies behind it, state its purpose, cite problem areas when appraising and counseling, explain "do's" and "don'ts" when conducting such a review, describe the procedural steps to be followed beforehand, explain how to prepare and to conduct the review, and cite how to follow through afterward.

WHAT IS THE PERFORMANCE APPRAISAL REVIEW?

The performance appraisal review is a meeting between two or more individuals for the purpose of presenting and explaining essential information about the job requirements, discussing and pooling ideas and arriving at recommendations for solving problems, setting objectives, developing action plans, and improving performance. It embodies investigations, discussions and communications between the administrator and the educator on matters which are of mutual interest and concern before decisions are made by either the educator or the administrator. The procedure for the performance appraisal review is characterized by an objective, unbiased discussion free of extraneous items, conducted in a climate free of emotional conflict. The technique of the performance appraisal review is designed to encourage participatory decision-making, effective thinking and frank expression by the parties involved in the review. When administrators use the performance appraisal review as a means for appraising and counseling, it produces improved and more acceptable decisions, it decreases the number and severity of school-related problems, and it satisfies the personal needs of the educators participating in important matters affecting them.

BASIC PHILOSOPHY BEHIND PERFORMANCE APPRAISAL REVIEW

1. The administrator can improve the achievement of his team, department, and school building system by periodically appraising the performance of his staff, and by appraising, directing, guiding, counseling and assisting at various appropriate times.

2. The administrator should manage and maintain the performance appraisal program as systematically as any other program. He must plan, organize, guide and control the activities of the program. Performance appraising review should be a more humane and effective way to performance evaluation and development.

3. Each educator should know (a) what is expected of him; (b) how he is doing; and (3) that he will be provided with assistance if he needs it.

4. The logical and most appropriate approach to the performance appraisal program is to assess performance in relation to results expected as previously agreed upon by the administrator and his staff. By so doing, the *what* and the *how much* was achieved by the educator are crystal clear.

5. For the purpose of improving the personal development of educators, it is necessary to determine why the performance was satisfactory. From this information the development and training program in an area of need can be ascertained.

6. There is much of value in the performance appraisal program since it is a system based on a mutual or joint process during which the educator evaluates himself and the administrator evaluates the educator. Improved performance results when the educator sees for himself where the fault lies and then does something about it.

7. The administrator should be familiar with the educator's achievements; however, it is possible that the educator can also enlighten the administrator on some points.

8. A great deal of the educator's performance development can be accomplished on the job.

9. All professional development is self-development. However, as the educator has the responsibility of achieving needed self-development, it is the responsibility of the administrator and the school system to provide appropriate counseling, opportunities, resources, and time for the educator's personal development.

10. The performance appraisal review should not only include assessment of the performance of the educator, but should also include a review of the services provided by the administrator to assist the educator in achieving his objectives. Just as the educator is self-appraising his own performance, so should the administrator assess *his* own performance with respect to his contributions to the educator's results.

11. A great deal of research has been performed which indicates that the performance appraisal review conference is of paramount importance for improving performance. The feedback which is exchanged between the supervisor and the educator is the basis upon which performance is achieved on, above or below plan. Research showed that when performance was reviewed frequently, either formally or informally, the following usually resulted:

a. The relationship between the supervisor and the educator improved.
b. The supervisors spent more time in improving the performance of their staff.
c. The objectives were achieved to a greater degree than if the post-appraisal conference did not exist or existed infrequently.
d. The teaching staff began to perceive their administrators as being helpful and considerate.
e. The administrators began to appreciate their staff more.
f. Administrators and teachers began to appreciate the program to a greater extent.
g. Teachers felt that their objectives were clearer.

PURPOSE OF PERFORMANCE
APPRAISAL REVIEW

Performance appraisal reviews are initiated for the following reasons:

1. *Reaching a mutual agreement on the key results analysis*

The very first task in goal setting is for the administrator to arrange a time and place to guide the educator in conducting a key results analysis. During this stage the administrator and the educator confer about the latter's job description. Each key area is discussed and analyzed, clarifications are made, and additional key areas may also be indicated. A job description is finally agreed to by both parties. Using the job description as the base, the educator is requested to segmentize his job in draft form onto the Individual Improvement Guide. Here he will list each key area, performance standards, methods for checking performance, and ways for improving performance. The draft is discussed and a final form mutually agreed to by the administrator and educator.

2. *Guiding and directing the educator in developing the School/Department Improvement Plan*

The next step is for the administrator and educator to meet for the purpose of developing the School/Department Improvement Plan. At this time, the administrator discusses the implications of long-range goals and the effect these goals will have on the plans of the department. Problems are also discussed which may be grounds for developing additional long-range goals or short-range objectives. Following this discussion, the educator drafts his proposed School/Department Improvement Plan and submits it to the administrator for review. A School Department Improvement Plan is subsequently mutually agreed to by both parties.

3. *Constructing an Individual Improvement Plan*

Using the School/Department Improvement Plan as a base, the educator develops his own improvement plans to achieve the long-range goals and short-range objectives of the school district and his department. A plan which is mutually agreed to by the administrator and the educator is formalized.

What Question Should be Stated During the Performance Appraisal Review:

During the review the following questions should be considered:

1. Are practical and realistic standards identified for each key area?
2. Are performance standards stated appropriately?
3. Have controls or methods for checking performance been identified for each key area and performance standard?
4. Are suggestions denoted for improving performance?
5. Were problem citations stated correctly?
6. Were the performance objectives stated using observable terms?

7. Were the objectives practical and realistic, yet challenging?
8. Do the objectives meet all of the requirements outlined in Chapter 6?
9. Will the action plan achieve the desired results?
10. Are target dates realistic?

One common fault which this author has observed when School MBO is being implemented is that some educators have a tendency to set low-risk-bearing goals. The administrator should be on the alert during this conference session for these low-risk-bearing goals, and should take this opportunity to negotiate more challenging goals. At times, however, an educator may have set his objectives too high (high-risk-setting goals). When this occurs, the administrator should counsel the educator to develop an objective more in line with reality.

PROBLEM AREAS WHEN APPRAISING AND COUNSELING

The primary problem area when appraising and counseling is that it is a human activity. A school is complex and by its very nature already beset with a variety of built-in human problems that occur when the administrator attempts to evaluate, judge, develop, modify and change the behavior of an educator. The degree to which the administrator's judgment is purely objective will determine the extent to which human judgment and personality problems can be decreased or even eliminated.

For years it has been known that the personality and expectations of the administrator create problems during the performance appraisal review. There are also problems which may occur as a result of the school environment which must be resolved one way or another: unclear objectives, lack of action plans for reaching objectives, lack of job classification, poor training in School MBO, lack of motivational techniques on the part of the administrator, and the reputations of both administrator and educator. The following constitute some potential problem areas in the performance appraisal review:

- Overcoming the natural biases of both administrator and educator.
- Evoking of characteristics and traits for the particular professional position.
- Reaching an agreement on the definition of each characteristic and trait.
- Deciding which characteristics and traits are to be appraised (a very touchy affair).
- Concentrating on performance in relation to results rather than dealing with judgments of educators.

However, most of the above pitfalls and problems can be avoided if the following antidotes are employed successfully:

- Administrator and educator mutually agree on objectives and record them in writing.
- Administrator and educator jointly agree on how performance will be evaluated.
- Administrator avoids criticizing and employs counseling and coaching techniques to get improved performance.
- Educator has supportive data for his self-appraisal report.
- Appraisal of the educator's performance is based on results achieved rather than on his personality.
- Educator develops his own objectives to support and reach the long-range goals established by the administrator.

Both administrators and educators should be familiar with the common pitfalls and problems associated with appraising and counseling. The chief school officer cannot effectively implement School MBO unless *all* educators make every attempt to circumvent the pitfalls and problems that are inherent in the program.

"DO'S AND DON'TS" WHEN CONDUCTING A PERFORMANCE APPRAISAL REVIEW

Do's:

1. Keep the individual or group on the subject, moving them forward in an orderly way through the discussion to arrive at specific ideas and solutions to problems.
2. If the conference lags, offer new ideas in order to give the educator a fresh look at the discussion or problem under consideration.
3. Be patient. If the discussion or questions are thought provoking, the educator will need sufficient time to think.
4. Be a good listener. This is done effectively by interjecting into the conversation: "Why?" "Tell me more about your objectives." "What do you hope to accomplish?"
5. Jot down comments and important points.
6. Summarize before the performance appraisal review terminates; it is always appropriate to recap mutual agreements.

Don't's:

1. Dictate overtly or implicitly by telling an individual or group what they should do or think.
2. Manipulate the educator by subtly trying to get predetermined conclusions.
3. Talk too much, if the purpose of the performance appraisal review is to get participation in the management of the affairs of the school. The administrator should talk less and listen more.
4. Display bias for your own ideas and suggestions by subtly getting the educator to react favorably to your recommendations.
5. Resort to phrases such as "You haven't . . . ," "I suppose you would agree . . . ," "I disagree with you . . . ."

THE PRELIMINARY STEPS BEFORE THE PERFORMANCE APPRAISAL REVIEW

Procedures and skill for conducting performance appraisal review will vary with the administrator according to the time available before, during, and after the review. The following are preliminary steps which should take place before conducting any review of performance.

Step I. Review All Essentials

Before the review and particularly during the periodic assessment of performance, the administrator should have consulted his notes from the previous review session. He should also review all notes made during the educator's observation. The administrator should review all of the available information at his disposal in order to ask the appropriate questions. During this phase of the preparation for the review, the administrator who is conducting the review should do his homework thoroughly.

Step II. Plan for the Performance Appraisal Review

The nature and amount of planning depends largely on two factors. They are:

1. Whether the administrator initiates it or is informed of it in sufficient time to permit planning.
2. Having done sufficient advance thinking about the problem, the administrator can spend his time during the conference listening, probing, and observing.

Step III. Notify the Educator About the Performance Appraisal Review

It is always appropriate to give the educator a reminder notice about the performance appraisal review, even though the administrator may be certain that the educator is aware of the review. When formulating the notice, the time, place, approximate duration and reason for the review should be spelled out. Some administrators have been known to use review notification as a psychological weapon by omitting the reason for the meeting. The educator who gets a notice without a declaration of the reason tends to take a negative point of view and often wonders, "What have I done now?" *In School MBO this sort of psychological warfare has no place.*

Step IV. Set the Stage for the Performance Appraisal Review

A successful review depends in part on a suitable setting. Some items which should be considered are:

1. *Privacy and comfortable environment.*

Whenever possible the review should be held in a private office with comfortable chairs and table. The author brings to mind one administrator who ordered a couch and a coffee table for his office to conduct meetings not only with teachers, but also with irate parents. Sometimes coffee is served by the administrator to relax the educator. Some administrators may prefer to conduct the conference in the privacy of a place away from the school setting.

2. *An atmosphere of leisure.*

There should be sufficient time to conduct the performance appraisal review. The review can usually be completed within one to two hours.

3. *Interruptions.*

Interruptions can seriously affect the review by destroying the continuity which has developed as a result of the interaction between the administrator and educator. In view of this it is desirable to provide for holding telephone calls and messages for the duration of the review. It may be advisable to post a sign indicating "In Conference—Do Not Disturb" on the office where the review is being conducted.

PREPARING FOR THE PERFORMANCE APPRAISAL REVIEW

The administrator is likely to conduct a successful performance appraisal review when he is well prepared attitudinally as well as intellectually.

1. Be objective in appraising the performance of the educator. Evaluate results achieved against results expected in specific "observable" terms. At this time, existing circumstances or emergencies which prevented anticipated results should be considered.

2. When analyzing the educator's performance, base it on observations which are derived from watching, listening and inquiring for the purpose of getting complete and accurate information.

3. Keep alert for important factors in the work situation which give insight into the educator's on-the-job performance.

4. Develop an effective way for recording the educator's performance, so that this can be used as a gauge for analyzing and evaluating.

5. The administrator should evaluate not only the performance of the educator, but also his own, in terms of how the educator is being assisted in meeting his objective.

CONDUCTING THE PERFORMANCE APPRAISAL REVIEW

1. After the administrator breaks the ice, the first subject to be discussed during the review should be a comparison of the results expected with results achieved. By reviewing the educator's outcome section of the improvement plans, this can be fairly easily accomplished. The administrator's role is to assist the educator in pinpointing areas of low achievement. He also guides the review so that definite conclusions are reached, and in the end the educator is well aware of his standing with the administrator.

2. The administrator should encourage the educator to do most of the talking at the review. It is the educator's development with which the administrator should be concerned; therefore, the administrator should provide the impetus that motivates the educator to speak freely. The administrator must remember that his primary role is to coach, to guide and to assist the educator in achieving his objectives.

3. The discussion of the objectives should develop from pertinent information so that the administrator and educator mutually agree on specific objectives to be achieved by the next performance appraisal review. It may be necessary to convene other meetings in order to provide more time for gathering essential data to arrive at appropriate objectives.

4. Documentation is not a dominant feature of the performance appraisal review; however, notes must be taken so that there is a mutual understanding of the matters discussed.

5. One copy of the improvement plan should be given to the educator; a copy should be retained by the administrator.

During the performance appraisal review, each objective and standard which was mutually agreed to is reviewed. To omit reviewing an objective cannot be condoned and is without justification. During this and subsequent reviews of performance the educator will be responsible for assessing *all* of the objectives which he set for himself.

During this performance appraisal review, the following should take place:

a. The educator evaluates his progress on the objective which he established for himself.
b. The validity of the original objective is evaluated by the administrator and educator.
c. Necessary modification of the improvement plans is made to make them more practical and realistic.
d. New objectives and action plans are added for the next periodic assessment conference.

This review should terminate with the administrator and educator mutually agreeing to the overall assessment of the performance during the period in question. This evaluation, like subsequent periodic evaluations, should be based entirely on results achieved in relation to results expected; personality should not be a factor. Exceptions to this rule are permitted only when personal traits are interfering with the educator's performance of his objectives.

CONCLUDING THE PERFORMANCE APPRAISAL REVIEW

The end of a review is very important if only because of impressions which may modify the educator's attitude.

The administrator should summarize the main points covered during the discussion and emphasize those items on which there was agreement. If the review was called by the educator in order to help him arrive at a decision, the administrator merely gives the pro's and con's for his decision.

It is usually professional courtesy to thank the educator for his time.

The administrator and educator should agree to close the review session at a mutually agreeable time.

REVIEWING AND EVALUATING THE PERFORMANCE APPRAISAL REVIEW

When the performance appraisal review has terminated, the wise administrator should carefully review his notes and mentally check through the review to assess his effectiveness as a coach or counselor and/or problem solver. In this process he should review what went wrong and what went right, reflecting on what he can do in the next review to improve his effectiveness as an administrator. Some administrators enjoy writing a self-evaluation report and periodically referring to this report to gauge the progress made in becoming more efficient.

FOLLOWING UP AFTER THE PERFORMANCE APPRAISAL REVIEW

Time has a tendency to slip by unnoticed, erasing the results of the best of reviews, therefore, maintaining a program for following up the performance appraisal review is not only important to an effective system of School MBO, it is essential. The following are some "action" areas for the effective administrator to bear in mind:

1. Observe the educator's performance and progress in the fulfillment of his objectives as they occur. Because the School MBO approach erases much of the fear in evaluating performance, most educators will accept and gladly welcome the administrator's evaluation.

2. The administrator should comment instantly on good performance and progress as soon as it is noticed. This is an extremely powerful way of motivating and developing a teacher.

3. Correct failure, when possible, in the form of demonstration and discussion. Discussions should take place immediately, thoroughly and constructively so that the educator will learn how to handle the problem mentioned.

Correction by demonstration and discussion is not as effective as directing improvement because it can lead to fear and discouragement. However, it does have its time and place in many educational situations.

4. Educators should be encouraged to perform satisfactorily. Old habits have a way of recurring. In order to effect desirable change, the administrator must constantly provide words of encouragement. However, the following must be considered:

a. Administrators should recognize that an encouragement becomes ineffective if no progress is made.

b. Administrators should always attempt to stimulate progress in order to prevent discouragement on the part of the teacher.

c. Administrators should commend the educator's performance even though it may not be up to his best performance. Any type of improved performance should be recognized by the administrator. The administrator should discuss the performance with the educator in order to assist in improving the current performance.

d. Administrators should remember to compliment competent performance and progress with objectives; an educator is likely to strive to achieve more difficult objectives when he is reasonably sure that his efforts are recognized.

5. The administrator should make it policy to follow up counseling by periodically reviewing the total picture with the educator, modifying broader goals if they become necessary.

6. The administrator should always keep his commitments and make certain that the educator does likewise.

SUMMARY

Performance appraisal review is a meeting between two or more individuals for the purpose of presenting and explaining essential information about the job requirements, discussing and pooling ideas and arriving at recommendations for solving problems, setting objectives, developing action plans, and improving performance.

The purposes of the performance appraisal review are: (1) Reaching a mutual agreement on the key results analysis; (2) Guiding and directing the educator in developing School/Department Improvement Plans; (3) Constructing an Individual Improvement Plan.

The following questions should be asked during the performance appraisal review: (1) Are practical and realistic standards identified for each key area? (2) Are performance standards stated appropriately? (3) Have controls or methods for checking performance been identified for each key area and performance standards? (4) Are suggestions denoted for improving performance? (5) Were problem citations stated correctly? (6) Were the performance objectives stated using observable terms? (7) Were the objectives practical and realistic, yet challenging? (8) Do the objectives meet all of the necessary requirements? (9) Will the action plan achieve the desired results? (10) Are target dates realistic?

The preliminary steps before the performance appraisal review are: Step I, Review all essentials; Step II, Plan for the performance appraisal review; Step III, Notify the educator about the performance appraisal review; Step IV, Set the stage for the performance appraisal review.

Prepare for the performance appraisal review by: (1) being objective in appraising performance; (2) basing results on observations, listening and inquiry; (3) keeping alert for important factors in the working situation which give insight into the educator's on-the-job performance; (4) evaluating his staff members' performance and his own.

Conducting the performance appraisal review should involve: (1) reviewing the educator's performance; (2) encouraging the educator to do most of the talking; (3) discussing pertinent information on specific objectives; (4) taking notes; (5) making three copies of performance appraisal review statement.

The administrator should conduct the performance appraisal review by summarizing or requesting that the educator summarize the main points mutually agreed to in the review. No review is complete unless an effort is made to follow up on the activities and recommendations made during the review.

NINE

Applying the
Key Results Analysis

There is a general belief that most administrators, supervisors, and teachers know what is expected of them in terms of results even though it may not be indicated in writing. "After all," commented one superintendent, "he has been the business manager of this school district for ten years. If he doesn't know what is expected of him now, he'll never know." In practice, many thousands of educators are unclear about the results expected of them and these doubts are the primary cause for insecurity, conservatism and lack of accountability commonly associated with educators. To erase these doubts, the author recommends that each educator be responsible for conducting a key results analysis; that is, analyze his job in terms of identifying each important task, set performance standards, devise control techniques, and render suggestions for improving performance for each task.

DEFINING KEY RESULTS ANALYSIS

Conducting a key results analysis is the process whereby an educator analyzes his job to determine key or major tasks which will have a significant impact on the success of his position. Once the key tasks have been identified and performance standards set, methods for checking performance and suggestions for improving performance (if any) are indicated for each key task. An Individual Improvement Guide is used to record the key results analysis.

The Individual Improvement Guide is a diagnostic instrument for determining the structure's effectiveness. It is especially of value in identifying if:

1. There is proper delegation of responsibility and authority.
2. Objectives (standards) of educators match, or are in line with, organizational goals and objectives.
3. There is confusion between jobs.
4. There are too many levels in the school organizational structure, causing poor communication network.
5. There is a missing function.

Each educator prepares his own key results analysis, with the School MBO advisor to guide him through the mechanics. The initial draft is usually the responsibility of the educator; the draft is subsequently reviewed, discussed, modified, amended, and mutually agreed upon in a conference attended by the educator, his immediate superior and the advisor.

If a disagreement should occur in the conference, provision should be made for a third "neutral" party to mediate. This could be an administrator or supervisor in the central administration office or an outsider.

USING THE JOB DESCRIPTION AS AN INSTRUMENT FOR CONDUCTING KEY RESULTS ANALYSIS

The educator's first step toward improving his performance is to demonstrate a basic understanding of his job: the purpose, scope, responsibilities and working relationships. The job description is a summary of the important facets of a person's job. It is a document intended to clarify the basic purpose of a position, the duties and responsibilities, and the boundaries of its authority.

The following is a recommended format for developing a job description:

Position Title:

The functional activity of the position should be indicated here, such as superintendent of schools, director of elementary education, special education teacher, etc.

Reports to:

Indicated here should be the title of the immediate supervisor of the position.

Broad Function:

Listed here should be a tersely written summary of the responsibilities of the position.

Principal Responsibility:

Such responsibility should be clearly and concisely written and in logical sequence. Grandiose terms which add nothing to the statements should be avoided. Each responsibility should be written in keeping with a consistent format. Beginning each responsibility with an action verb is highly recommended. This helps to avoid using unnecessary terms and delineates each principal responsibility of the job in observable terms.

A job description which follows the above recommended format is indicated in Exhibit 9-1.

JOB DESCRIPTION

POSITION TITLE: Assistant Superintendent for Business Affairs

REPORTS TO: Superintendent of Schools

BROAD FUNCTION: To manage the business affairs and facilities of the school district and to ensure that they are administered in the most efficient and economical manner possible.

PRINCIPAL RESPONSIBILITIES: In achieving his basic objectives, he continually develops and implements:

1. Timely preparation and control of school budget.
   a. Supervise the preparation of the annual budget and provide assistance.
   b. Control all expenditures made against the budget by giving final approval to purchase orders.
   c. Approve bills for payment and present them to the Board of Education for final approval.
2. Sound purchasing systems.
   a. Prepare announcements for public bidding and after analysis of the bids, make recommendations to the Board of Education for award of purchase contracts.
3. Efficient borrowing and effective investment of school funds.
   a. Make arrangements for borrowing money and investing district funds subject to Board approval.
4. Adequate negotiations assistance.
   a. Provide staff assistance in collective negotiations with the various bargaining units of district employees.
5. Effectual recruitment program.
   a. Make final arrangements for hiring of non-teaching personnel including liaison with the County Civil Service Commission.

EXHIBIT 9-1

6. District-wide census program.
   a. Supervise the taking of the annual school district census of young people through age 18.
7. Provide adequate insurance coverage for all phases of the school district operations.
8. Punctual submission of required reports.
   a. Prepare all required local and state financial, business and statistical reports.

EXHIBIT 9-1 (continued)

A job description should be available for each member of the school district. If a job description is not available, one should be written immediately before proceeding with the key results analysis. If a job description is available, it would be wise to review it for possible revisions, modifications, and updating.

Once the job description is written in draft form and submitted, discussed, amended (if need be) and mutually agreed to by the immediate supervisor, the second step toward conducting key results analysis involves completing the Individual Improvement Guide. An abbreviated version of such a guide appears on the following pages (Exhibit 9-2).

IDENTIFYING THE COMPONENTS OF INDIVIDUAL IMPROVEMENT GUIDE FOR
ADMINISTRATIVE AND SUPERVISORY POSITIONS

There are six sections to the Individual Improvement Guide:

Section I—Main Purpose of Job

Indicated here are the main contributions of the particular job to the efficient operation of the school system.

Section II—Position in Organization

Listed here is the immediate supervisor of the educator, that is, the person he is directly responsible to or the person who evaluates his performance. Also listed here is the staff that is directly supervised by the educator.

INDIVIDUAL IMPROVEMENT GUIDE

⊂══▷◁══▷◁══▷

Dr. Warner Davis
_____
ADMINISTRATOR / SUPERVISOR

Assistant Superintendent for Business Affairs
_____
POSITION

July 10, 19--
_____
DATE

GODARD PUBLIC SCHOOLS

HAVEN, NEW YORK

EXHIBIT 9-2

I. Main Purpose of Job

(State the main contribution of the job for the efficient operation of the school system)

> To administer the business operation of the school district in order to achieve maximum efficiency, maximum economy and a high standard of service to the superintendent and his staff of administrators and teachers.

II. Position in Organization

    a.) Directly responsible to:

        Superintendent

    b.) Staff directly supervised:

        Two senior account clerks   Three summer clerical workers
        One stenographer
        One account clerk

IV. Key Tasks

Key Area	Description of Key Task (main sub-division of the job)	Standard of Performance (results Targets)
Preparation and control of school budget	1.1 Assist the superintendent to prepare budget	1.1 A budget which provides for all required district expenditures without being bloated with unnecessary appropriations.
	1.2 Give final approval to purchase orders	1.2 Controlling expenditures to within. 2% or more under budget appropriations.
	1.3 Approve bills for payment	1.3 Avoid excess payments to vendors or making payments to wrong vendors.
Purchasing Systems	2.1 Supervise competitive bidding process for goods and services being bought by school district	2.1 Adhere to legal guidelines set by general municipal law and obtain quotations from at least four vendors on each public bid.
	2.2 Approve routine purchase orders	2.2 Weed out any improper purchase orders.

V. Personal Activities:

(List those activities actually performed by you and not delegated. Items included here will be part of the Key Tasks)

    All key tasks except 4.1 and 6.2

EXHIBIT 9-2 (continued)

III. Scope of the Job
(indicate your total responsibilites in terms of staff, materials and facilities)

```
Personnel:    5 full-time
              3 part-time

Budget allocation (1972-73)

    Personnel              $82,806
    Equipment                4,880
    Supplies                 1,000
    Service contracts       12,675
Postage                      1,640
Travel conference              200
Total                    $103,201
```

Method of Checking Performance	Suggestions for Performance Improvement
1.1 Annual check of financial report for line item over expenditure and under expenditure	1.1 Begin budget preparation early (in fall).
1.2 Same as 1.1	1.2 Consult previous year's performance figures.
1.3 Experience check for 60-day period after payment of bills	1.3 Provide in-service training for accounts payable section.
2.1 Visual check of bid announcements and bids received	2.1 Enlarge bidders' lists on all commodities and services.
2.2 Maintain file of cancelled purchase orders	2.2 Review legal restrictions with originating departments.

VI. Limits of Authority.
(Items in this section will normally concern some or all of the following: physical resources, personnel and financial commitments.)

Perform within budget limitations.

EXHIBIT 9-2 (continued)

IV. Key Tasks continued.

Key	Description of Key Task (main sub-division of the job)	Standard of Performance (results Targets)
Borrowing and Investment of School Funds	3.1 Prepare a cash flow analysis for each fiscal year	3.1 Come within 10% accuracy month by month, for cash flow figures.
	3.2 Recommend to the Board when and how much to borrow on a tax anticipation note	3.2 Manage funds to the district does not have to make use of a tax anticipation note for the first month and, hopefully, for the first two months of the school year.
	3.3 Recommend to the Board when and how much to invest in Certificates of Deposit	3.3 Obtain an interest rate higher than that provided in the district savings account.
Negotiation Assistance	4.1 Prepare salary and fringe benefit studies for use by negotiating team	4.1 Have studies ready for chief negotiator by Dec. 1, 19--
Recruitment	5.1 Supervise in-district personnel processing in hiring non-teaching staff	5.1 Non-teaching staff not subject to falling off payroll, missing health insurance benefits, etc.
	5.2 Follow civil service regulations in hiring non-teaching staff	5.2 No criticisms from the Civil Service Commission for failure to follow regulations.
Census Taking	6.1 Develop a system for taking the school census	6.1 Locate over 95% of the district's residents up to 18 years of age.
	6.2 Supervise census crew and make sure it follows the proper census procedures	6.2 Less than 5% error on cards coded for computer run on census reports.

Insurance Coverage	7.1 Maintain adequate insurance coverage on the following:
	a. Personnel
	  1. Health
	  2. Dental
	  3. Life insurance
	b. Physical plant
	  1. Fire
	  2. Liability
	c. Transportation
	  1. All vehicles
		7.1 Institute automatic updated insurance coverage on all insurance policies.

EXHIBIT 9-2 (continued)

Method of Checking Performance	Suggestions for Performance Improvement
3.1 Monthly check of cash flow analysis vs. actual figures	3.1 Consult school business administrators who have a good record on cash flow.
3.2 Check against the experiences of the first two months of fiscal year	3.2 Plan for a modest surplus to carry into the new school year.
3.3 Monthly check on performance	3.3 Cultivate close relations with banking community as a source of suggestions on investments.
4.1 Check with chief negotiator after session to see if he is satisfied with information received	4.1 Begin the preparation of these studies soon as the new fiscal year begins.
5.1 Lack of complaints by staff	5.1 Review personnel procedures for the transmission of personnel changes and addition.
5.2 Failure of Civil Service to make any criticisms when payroll is certified	5.2 Use civil service check list for each appointment or termination.
6.1 Checking against federal census information	6.1 Attempt an automobile canvass of houses in district to make certain that all houses are accounted for.
6.2 Figure the percentage of input errors annually	6.2 Provide closer supervision over census crew.
7.1 Insurance policy provision for automatic updating insurance coverage	7.1 Obtain competitive insurance rates on all insurance coverage. Submit to superintendent for his consideration.

EXHIBIT 9-2 (continued)

Section III—Scope of the job

Here the educator should indicate the total responsibilities of his job in terms of budgetary expenditures in the areas of personnel, materials, and facilities. At this point, the educator should get a better insight into his job in terms of financial and educational accountability.

Section IV—Key Tasks

This section, which is probably the most important part of the guide, has five columns, as described below:

KEY RESULTS AREAS

In this column are listed the key areas of the educator's position. Each key area should be developed by the administrator for major job functions within departments which he is responsible for fulfilling.

The key results analysis is the initial and perhaps the most important step toward improving the performance of an individual or department, a school and a school district. The analysis must be performed systematically, with care, and sometimes under the direct supervision of the advisor. Each key results analysis should meet the following criteria.

1. Each item should be relevant, in that it is directly concerned with the success or failure of the job as a whole.
2. Each key results area selected should be reasonably independent, so that unnecessary overlapping judgments do not occur.
3. Each item selected should be assessable in terms of effective performance of the job-holder.
4. The total number of result areas for a job should not be so large that trivial items are introduced, nor should the number be so small that excessive generalization occurs.[1]

Examples:

1. *Administrator's Performance*
   (The ability to recruit, train and retain a loyal and effective administration and supervisory team and to utilize it in an effective manner.)
2. *School Budget*
   (The ability to prepare the annual school budget.)
3. *School Census*
   (The ability to take, analyze and report annually the school census to superintendents.)

---

[1]John W. Humble, *Management Objectives in Action*, McGraw-Hill, New York, 1970, p. 115.

4. *Testing Program*

(The ability to develop and administer group testing programs and coordinate them with individual testing programs.)

DESCRIPTION OF KEY TASKS

In this column are listed descriptions of key tasks which will have a significant impact on the success of the educator's position.

Each administrator must be clear about the *results* he is expected to achieve, in line with school goals and objectives, or he may waste his time and energy in unimportant tasks. Moreover, there will be no agreed base against which to review performance and on which to develop a training program. Although most boards of education assume that their educators already know what is expected of them, many in fact do not. The traditional job descriptions are usually too generalized, lengthy, and often incomplete, confusing activities and failing to differentiate unimportant tasks from important ones.

The key task statement should be a precise, unequivocal description of a key task, phrased in such a way that it defines the essential action accurately, leading to results. If the task has been clearly described, completing the following sentence should enable an effective standard of performance to emerge: "This task is being well done when. . . ."

A number of rules for writing tasks are given:

Rule 1: State only key tasks—the 20 per cent of the tasks that produce 80 per cent of the results.
Rule 2: Do not produce woolly or indefinite statements; use precise and unequivocal language.
Rule 3: Keep descriptions brief.
Rule 4: The key tasks should lead naturally into results projected.
Rule 5: The tasks described must be those of the educator.[2]

STANDARDS OF PERFORMANCE

Performance standards are developed for each key task. A performance standard is a statement describing a condition that will exist when the projected result is being achieved.

Different categories of performance standards are identified:

(a) Measured or quantitative.
(b) Preventative, e.g., when an undesirable result does not occur.

---

[2]Ibid, p. 199.

(c) Judged or qualitative—standard depends on precise working rather than quantitative measures.

(d) Shared—where the achievement of a result target is a joint responsibility.

A number of rules for defining standards are established:

Rule 1: Performance standards must be statements of results or conditions, not descriptions of actions taken.

Rule 2: They should answer the question: "What level of results will be achieved if the job is being well performed?"

Rule 3: Ask: "Would failure to reach this level of performance be a serious matter?"

Rule 4: The performance standard set should not be less than the current level of results being achieved (apart from very exceptional cases).

Performance standards are elaborated upon in Chapter 4.

METHODS OF CHECKING PERFORMANCE

Listed here should be check points for monitoring performance. The immediate supervisor must be supplied with feedback to determine if performance is above, on, or below plan.

Check points should be available to show both the administrator and his educator how each part of the job is going. When this information is not available, or is ambiguous, or late, the educator will be expected to suggest what he needs to control his job.

The following are some specific measurement devices or methods which are used to check performance:

1. Personal observation or inspection.
2. Daily, weekly, monthly status reports.
3. PERB reports.
4. Program schedule reports.
5. Daily program meetings; verbal status reports.
6. Charts.
7. Reports from departments.
8. Written assignment instructions, returned with action taken checked off or annotated.
9. Daily activity report card. "This is what I did today. . . ."

10. Problem reports, verbal or written.
11. Permanent bar charts.
12. Log book.
13. Control charts.

Monitoring performance is discussed in Chapter 5.

SUGGESTIONS FOR PERFORMANCE IMPROVEMENT

This column pertains to any information or data which will lead to the improvement of performance by the educator, that is, comments on what needs to be done to achieve higher performance standards and by whom.

Examples:

Performance Standard	Method of Checking Performance	Suggestions for Improving Performance
(80% of new teaching staff prove to be satisfactory)	(Staff's performance review reports)	Improved teaching staff application forms required
(Teaching staff agree that weaknesses are identified and suitable training defined)	(Teaching staff records)	Require formal periodic performance meeting with training administrator

Section V—Personal Activities

Listed here are those activities which the educator is directly responsible for achieving and for the results of which he is therefore solely accountable.

Section VI—Limits of Authority

Indicated here should be the constraints imposed on the educator in terms of physical resources, personnel and financial commitments, policy and procedures.

DEVELOPING INDIVIDUAL IMPROVEMENT GUIDE FOR TEACHING POSITIONS

The Individual Improvement Guide for teaching positions contains the name of the teacher, description of the position, date, key task areas, performance standards, methods for checking performance, suggestions for improving performance and a comment section.

The following are the procedural steps for conducting a key results analysis via Individual Improvement Guide for teaching positions:

1—A committee of teachers meet for the purpose of formulating job description. This job description is basically a performance criteria guide which describes general assumption of main areas of concern regarding effective teaching performance.
2—The job description is mutually agreed to by the teaching staff and immediate supervisor or principal and becomes a contract between said parties.
3—Each teacher uses the job description to develop his own key results analysis which is recorded on the Individual Improvement Guide.
4—Each Individual Improvement Guide is mutually agreed to by the immediate supervisor.
5—Each teacher during individual or collective efforts exerts himself to perform in accordance with the Individual Improvement Guide.

ALL SUBSEQUENT STEPS INVOLVE APPRAISING PERFORMANCE WHICH HAS BEEN DISCUSSED PREVIOUSLY.

An example of a job description and an Individual Improvement Guide are illustrated in Exhibits 9-3 and 9-4.

JOB DESCRIPTION

POSITION TITLE: Elementary Teacher

REPORTS TO: Team Leader

BROAD FUNCTION: The elementary teacher manages his classroom in such a way that its goals and objectives support and amplify those established by the board of education. To accomplish those ends, he

---

EXHIBIT 9-3

continually plans, presents subject matter in an effective manner and maintains an effective class environment.

PRINCIPAL RESPONSIBILITIES: Within the approved limits of Board policy as delineated by the team leader, assistant elementary principal and the principal, the elementary teacher is responsible for the following:

Planning:
1. Participates in setting long-range goals for the school.
2. Formulates short-range objectives for improving performance.
3. Plans for and meets the needs of individual students.
4. Coordinates planning and preparation of classroom and material.

Presentation of Subject Matter:
1. Presents subject matter in a logical form, stressing the higher thought processes.
2. Demonstrates mastery of subject matter for grade and subject.
3. Varies instructional materials for grade and subject.
4. Provides a variety of learning materials and equipment to encourage self-directed learning.

Classroom Environment:
1. Maintains a favorable classroom environment (psychological) for learning.
2. Maintains a classroom environment (physical) conducive to learning.
3. Provides structure within a "free" environment for learning.
4. Demonstrates fairness and kindness in dealing with students.
5. Makes effective and differentiated assignments.
6. Demonstrates a respect for the integrity of the individual pupil's personality.
7. Demonstrates intelligent economy in the use of materials and equipment.
8. Seeks to instill moral and ethical values.
9. Is receptive to intelligent educational experimentation.
10. Displays a contagious enthusiasm for knowledge.
11. Assigns homework with respect to the students' out-of-school time.
12. Initiates problem-solving conference to solve student or class problems.
13. Communicates effectively with students.

Staff Relationship:
1. Works cooperatively with staff members toward attaining the goals accepted for the schools and team.

EXHIBIT 9-3 (continued)

2. Participates willingly with study groups and curriculum committee.
3. Displays loyalty to the school and community.
4. Works cooperatively with teachers and administratively towards attaining objectives of the school district, school building and team.

Professional Enhancement:
1. Takes personal responsibility for individual professional growth.
2. Participates in professional organizations.
3. Initiates a variety of personal development activities.

Parents and Community Relations:
1. Takes appropriate action in regard to parents' requests, complaints and concerns.
2. Displays a willingness to explain classroom procedures and educational programs.
3. Displays effectiveness in parent-teacher conferences.
4. Attends Parent-Teacher Association meetings.
5. Avoids argumentation or defensive attitude with parents.
6. Cooperates effectively with parents on conference follow-up.
7. Participates effectively in a number of community affairs or projects.

Exhibit 9-3 (continued)

The following are some comments denoted by some administrators who have implemented School MBO for the first time:

"The Administrator Improvement Guide was helpful in that it requires the individual to focus on his responsibilities for the purpose of delineating them and examining them in order of their priority."

"I, myself, never realized the many tasks involved in being an administrator until I put them down on paper. There should be no question in anyone's mind as to what is involved in a particular job or how to go about improving yourself or your department when it is expressed clearly and concisely in writing and in booklet form."

"The improvement guide and plans will be of great help to me in the future. Even the job description was new to me and I now see the need for one; especially in my school where one's duties are not always clear."

The Individual Improvement Guide should never be considered in isolation. Each Guide is a component of the wider analysis of the total school district. In effect, improvement guides are diagnostic instruments for evaluating the school's effectiveness.

INDIVIDUAL IMPROVEMENT GUIDE

Ms. Valdmir Cummins
ADMINISTRATOR / SUPERVISOR

Elementary Teacher
POSITION

March 19--
DATE

GODARD PUBLIC SCHOOLS

HAVEN, NEW YORK

EXHIBIT 9-4

IV. Key Tasks continued.

Key Area	Description of Key Task (main sub-division of the job)	Standard of Performance (results Targets)
Planning	3.1 Participate in setting long range goals for the school.	3.1 Assist in needs assessment program.
	3.2 Formulate short range objectives for improving performance.	3.2 Maintain school/department and Individual improvement plans.
	3.3 Plans for and meets the needs of individual students.	3.3 a. Maintain a log on each student b. Assign classwork in accordance with needs as indicated in log book.
	3.4 Coordinates planning and preparation of classroom and material.	3.4 Meet daily 1 hour before classes begin to coordinate day's activities.
Subject Matter Presentation	4.1 Presents subject matter in a logical form, stressing the higher thought process.	4.1 Use behavioral objectives in all subject matter.
	4.2 Demonstrate mastery of subject matter.	4.2 Write and publish a scholarly article on elementary education.
	4.3 Varies instructional materials.	4.3 In accordance with learning patterns: a. structured b. semi-structured c. self-directed
Classroom Environment	5.1 Maintain a favorable classroom environment (psychological) for learning.	5.1 a. Avoid admonishing students in front of peers. b. Solve problems via problem solving conference.
	5.2 Maintains a classroom environment (physical) conducive to learning	5.2 a. Provide ample desk, chairs and tables. b. Establish a library corner with couch, lamp and rug.
	5.3 Provides structure within a "free" environment for learning.	5.3 Establish learning patterns and prescribe instruction according to: a. structured b. semi-structured c. self-directed
	5.4 Demonstrate fairness and kindness in dealing with students.	5.4 Permit students to formulate their own classroom rules.

EXHIBIT 9-4 (continued)

Method of Checking Performance	Suggestions for Performance Improvement
3.1 Needs Assessment Report.	3.1 Attend a workshop on needs assessment program given by the State Department of Education.
3.2 School/Department and Individual Improvement Plans.	
3.3 Teacher's log on students.	3.3 Students should maintain their own log.
3.4 Written daily schedule.	3.4 Read more in this area.
4.1 Instructional plans.	4.1 Read Lewis, James, Jr., _A Systems Approach to Developing Behavioral Objectives_, National Association for the Individualization of Instruction, Wyandanch, N.Y. 19--
4.2 Forward copy of manuscript to principal.	
4.3 Instructional plans, classroom absenteeism, and teacher's log on students.	4.3 Committee should be formed to develop instructional materials for the various learning patterns.
5.1 Classroom observation and informal student survey.	5.1 Visit class whereby the teacher uses the problem-solving conference.
5.2 Classroom observation.	
5.3 Instructional plans.	5.3 Read more in this area.
	5.5 Request federal aid coordinator to see funds for organizing a committee to develop differential assignments during the summer vacation.
5.4 Report from teacher.	
5.5 Teacher's log on students.	

EXHIBIT 9-4 (continued)

SUMMARY

Conducting a key results analysis is the process whereby an educator analyzes his job to determine key or major tasks which will have a significant impact on the success of his job. The educator's first step toward improving his performance is to acquire a clear understanding of his job: the purpose, scope, responsibility and working relationships. The job description should contain: (1) Position Title; (2) Report to; (3) Broad Function; (4) Principal Responsibility.

Once the job description has been written or rewritten, the educator should proceed to complete his key results analysis using the Individual Improvement Guide. There are six sections to this Guide: (1) Main Purpose of Job; (2) Position in Organization; (3) Scope of Job; (4) Key Tasks; (5) Personal Activities; (6) Limits of Authority. The Guide should never be considered in isolation. It should be seen as a component of wider analysis of the total school district.

TEN

Developing Improvement Plans for Continued Progress

When the final draft of the Individual Improvement Guide has been completed and a copy submitted to the educator's supervisor, the next step for improving personnel effectiveness through School MBO is a meeting between the educator and his immediate supervisor for the purpose of discussing and listing priorities and problems which need solving. First on the agenda should be a discussion of the implications of the long-range goals established by the board of education and superintendent for the individual's job and position. *Long-range goals always receive first priority in developing any improvement plans.* Once the educator is clear as to what is expected of him in terms of attaining long-range goals, further discussion should take place using the views of administrators, supervisors and teachers and the suggestions indicated on the Individual Improvement Guides as the basis for developing School/Department Improvement Plan and Individual Improvement Plan. The rationale of this chapter is to explain the necessary steps for completing improvement plans.

CONSTRUCTING THE SCHOOL AND DEPARTMENT IMPROVEMENT PLAN

After the critical analysis has been concluded and the priorities have been decided, the administrators and supervisors must consider how each improvement area is going to be achieved in light of the time and resources available. To perform this feat, each principal or department head is required to develop a plan for improving his respective school or department, using the School/Department Improvement Plan. An abbreviated version of the School/Department Plan appears in Exhibit 10-1.

Each plan must be approved by the educator's immediate supervisor. Modifications, deletions, revisions, or additions are made on the plan and a copy is forwarded to the supervisor.

The following are the essential progressive steps for developing the School/Department Improvement Plan:

Step I—Identify the Area for Improvement

Listed here is the area for which result is expected. In most cases this should be identical to the key area in the Individual Improvement Guide.

Step II—Outline the Problem

Indicated here should be a brief outline of the problem which necessitates the corrective action. The problem should indicate present conditions and the desired results.

Examples:

The percentage of students reading above the national average is 30% as compared to 70% for the surrounding school districts.

The percentage of students dropping out of school for the West High School is approximately 20%, as compared to 5% for the East High School.

The teacher turnover rate is 25%, which should be reduced to 10%.

Step III—Develop Performance Objectives

The principal or department head should develop a performance objective for solving each problem. Although Chapter 6 amplified the writing of performance objectives, the following are some guidelines:

1. Begin with the word "to" followed by an action verb.
2. Delineate a single key result to be accomplished.
3. Specify a target date for its accomplishment.
4. Be specific, quantitative, reasonable, and verifiable.
5. State "what" and "when."
6. Be realistic, attainable, and present a challenge.
7. Be consistent with basic school policies and procedures.

SCHOOL/DEPARTMENT IMPROVEMENT PLAN

GODARD High SCHOOLS
_____
SCHOOL/DEPARTMENT

Dr. John Wilkenson
_____
ADMINISTRATOR/SUPERVISOR

High School Principal
_____
POSITION

October 1, 19--
_____
DATE

GODARD PUBLIC SCHOOLS

HAVEN, NEW YORK

EXHIBIT 10-1

School/Department Improvement Plan

Date ___October 1,_____ 19_____

Area For Improvement	Problem (What's Wrong)	Objectives For Current Year	
		Main	Breakdown of Action
Student Safety	During 19-- the number of student accidents reported increased to 204, 101 more than preceding year.	To reduce student accidents from 204 to 100 by June 30,19--	1. At teachers' orientation, make teachers aware of problem, explain objective and elicit their support.
			2. Require all teachers to step out into hall between periods and monitor students' conduct.
			3. Assign teachers to hall duty before and after school hours.
			4. Coordinate hall duty assignments.
			5. Teachers having bus duty will attend orientation meeting.
			6. Alert coaches to pay closer attention to safety procedures.
			7. Distribute a quarterly report on safety from school nurse to each staff member .
			8. Assign additional teachers to supervise problem areas as per quarterly report.
			9. Make daily inspections of labs and shops to check safety procedures. Follow up if necessary.
			10. Construct a series of "bumps" in school parking lots to slow cars down.
			11. Purchase new desks for rooms 201 & 202
			12. All rooms not in use are to be locked by teacher.

EXHIBIT 10-1 (continued)

Administrator/Supervisor___Dr. John Wilkenson___

Position___High School Principal___

Target Date	Action By (Educator)	Outcome (Results, etc.)
Sept. 8, 19--	High school principal	
Sept. 9, 19--	High school principal and assistant principal	
Sept. 9, 19--	High school principal	
Sept. 9, 19--	Assistant principal	
Sept. 15, 19--	Assistant principal	
Sept. 20, 19--	Assistant principal	
Monday after termination of each quarter	Assistant principal	
Immediately upon need	Assistant principal	
Daily	Assistant principal	
December 1, 19--	Assistant superintendent for business	
Sept. 9, 19--	High school principal	
Sept. 9, 19--	Assistant principal	Above plan - The number of student accidents for the school year 19-- was reduced from 204 to 78 as indicated in the last quarterly report.

EXHIBIT 10-1 (continued)

School/Department Improvement Plan

Date ___October 1_____ 19_____

Area For Improvement	Problem (What's Wrong)	Objectives For Current Year	
		Main	Breakdown of Action
Organization	The board of education has established the following long-range goal: To implement school management by objectives throughout the school district by June 30, 19--	To implement the first phase of school management by objectives in Godard High School by June 30, 19--	1. Become adept in theory and practice to for installing school management by objectives. See Individual Improvement Plan. 2. Develop a time table for instituting school management by objectives. 3. Conduct critical analysis and set goals. 4. Develop or revise job descriptions. 5. Prepare key results analysis. 6. Reach a mutual agreement on department and individual improvememt plans. 7. Initiate performance appraisal review.

EXHIBIT 10-1 (continued)

Administrator/Supervisor___Dr. John Wilkenson___

Position___High School Principal___

Target Date	Action By (Educator)	Outcome (Results, etc.)
February 9, 19--	High school principal	On plan - All activities were achieved on or above plan as indicated by Individual Improvement Plan.
October 15, 19--	SMBO advisor and high school principal	Above plan - Time table was completed by October 1, 19--
November 1, 19--	All administrators and supervisors in high school assisted by SMBO advisor	On plan - Critical analysis was conducted and two long-range goals were established Re: Memo #7.
November 15, 19--	All administrators and supervisors in high school assisted by SMBO advisor	On plan - Job descriptions for administrators and supervisors were reviewed by SMBO advisor and high school principal. Modifications and revisions were also made.
December 20, 19--	All administrators and supervisors in high school assisted by SMBO advisor	On plan - Individual Improvement Guides have been reviewed by SMBO advisor and high school principal. Modifications and revisions have also been made and a copy of each administrator's and supervisor's Guide is retained in my files.
January 31, 19--	High school principal and all administrators and supervisors	On plan - All department and individual improvement plans have been mutually agreed to.
March 15, 19--	High school principal	On plan - Performance appraisal reviews have been conducted on all administrators and supervisors.

EXHIBIT 10-1 (continued)

Examples:

To develop a tentative language arts curriculum guide for grades 8-12 by March 31, 19——.

To develop a program of supervision and in-service training of teachers for the improvement of the institution by June 30, 19——.

(Additional examples of performance objectives are indicated in Chapter 6.)

Step IV—Construct a Step-by-Step Breakdown of Action Required

Delineated here is the process of breaking the objectives down into steps for effective accomplishment. The act of breaking down an objective is another means of validating it. There are eight recommended approaches to breaking down an objective for step-by-step accomplishment (more fully discussed in Chapter 7).

1. Study situation and select most appropriate method.
2. Gain agreement and support.
3. Develop the plan of action.
4. Project a timetable for achieving each activity in the action plan. (Please note: *This procedure is usually reserved for the next step.*)
5. Designate the person and activity to be initiated. (Please note: *Designating the person initiating the individual activity is usually reserved for the sixth procedural step.*)
6. Test and review.
7. Implement.
8. Follow up.

The following questions should be answered when breaking down an objective:

1. What important steps are necessary in order to achieve the results projected in the objective?
2. What priorities should be assigned to each essential step?
3. What detailed steps are necessary to support the important steps which have been developed?

Example:

Objective
To increase the number of third grade students on grade level in math from 10% to 30% by June 30, 19——, as indicated on state-wide survey test.

Step-by-Step Breakdown (target dates are omitted here) of Action Required
   1. Review and improve third grade math curriculum.
   2. Give daily instruction in math skills.
   3. Homework in math will be given at least four (4) times every week.
   4. Weekly tests will be given in math per class position in unit.
   5. A grade test will be given at the completion of every unit to determine level of grade mastered.
   6. There will be a daily review of skills taught.
   7. Tape recordings, dittos, and audio-visual aids will be composed by third grade teachers at different phases throughout each unit.
   8. Every third week there will be a grade assessment of the students' progress.
   9. After every unit test has been administered and evaluated by teachers of the grade, there will be a meeting of the building principal and director of math, along with the teachers, to determine accuracy of tests and results and to make any necessary recommendations.

Step V—Indicate Target Dates

A target date should be indicated for each step. This activity may be of little or no importance, or it may be the most critical step to be performed to reach the desired result. It may involve investigation, experimentation, or approximation.

Step VI—Identify the Person Responsible for Achieving Each Step of the Action Plan

Indicated here should be the name of the person or persons responsible for achieving each step of the action required to achieve the objective. It may be necessary at times to get the prior approval of the person who is being requested to perform a certain activity in the action plan.

Step VII—Review Performance

The appraisal of results should be indicated in the "outcome" column. Factors impeding desired achievement are identified and possible solutions of difficulties are discussed here.

Explanation for performance delay is presented and amendments to the School/Department Improvement Plan that are necessary to get on target to achieve the objective should also be recorded in this column.

The performance review covers:

1. A review of performance achieved against projected results.
2. An analysis of variances.
3. Action required in order to achieve objective.
4. The revision of objectives where necessary.
5. A clarification of all performance which is below plan, with an explanation as to what corrective action will be taken to achieve the objective.

The following are some examples of how results are recorded:

Above plan
Teachers' absentee rate has decreased from 50 days to 20 days for the period (well below the goal of 30 days).

On plan
Monthly reports on ESEA Title I expenditures have been and will continue to be submitted to Parents Advisory Council before the 15th of each month as planned.

Below plan
Only 14 classroom visitations were made during this period (projected plan was 20). The remaining four classroom visitations will be conducted during the next period. Absence for 22 days due to illness prevented the achievement of this objective. There should be no difficulty in achieving this objective as planned for the next period.

Amendment
Monitoring teacher performance in math should be performed on a bi-weekly basis instead of weekly.

DEVELOPING THE INDIVIDUAL IMPROVEMENT PLAN

When the School/Department Improvement Plan is completed and mutually agreed to by the parties concerned, an Individual Improvement Plan is broken down into a series of results required by the various educators within the department and then expressed in the form of the Individual Improvement Plan. An abbreviated version of the Individual Improvement Plan appears in Exhibit 10-2.

Once the Individual Improvement Plan is agreed to by the immediate supervisor, it becomes a vital component to the success of the individual school or department. The administrator and supervisor are committed to achieving the objectives and the immediate supervisor is committed to providing whatever assistance has been mutually agreed upon during the conference session. If changing conditions reduce the likelihood of achieving an objective, the educator must report the situation to his supervisor and alternative means should be found which are mutually agreeable.

The Individual Improvement Plan has the following characteristics:

—Coupled with the Individual Improvement Guide, it is the basis upon which each principal and department head understands what is expected of him in terms of individual results.
—Unlike the Individual Improvement Guide, the Individual Improvement Plan is relatively flexible and is subject to change if conditions or priorities change. The Individual Improvement Guide is relatively static, unless there is a change in the nature of the position.
—The content of the Individual Improvement Plan is derived from the School/Department Improvement Plan.
—The same form is often used to record personal development objectives for the individual.
—Individual Improvement Plan form is also used to record the individual's performance review.
—The performance review section is used for determining training objectives.

Although the steps for developing the Individual Improvement Plan are similar to the School/Department Improvement Plan, there are slight variations:

Step I—Identify the Key Result Areas for Improvement

Listed here are the major job functions which the administrator has overall responsibility for improving.

Step II—Cite the Improvement Action

Indicated here are the details of the performance objective which is projected to bring about the expected results.

Step III—Develop Step-by-Step Breakdown of Action Required

Delineated here is a breakdown of the activities (*action* plan) projected to reach the objective.

Step IV—Devise Target Dates

Indicated here are the projected dates for achieving the various activities in the action plan.

Step V—Identify Individual Responsibility (by whom?)

Cited here are the names of persons responsible for achieving individual activities in the action plan.

Step VI—Summarize the Performance Outcome

Specify here the performance outcome in terms of on-, above-, and below-plan performance, delays, or amendments.

SUMMARY

When the key results analysis has been completed and mutually agreed to by the parties concerned, the first step towards developing improvement plans involves a critical examination of all available data to determine needs and priorities. A review of the following data is recommended before developing improvement plans: (1) Needs Assessment Report; (2) Past and present long-range goals and short-range objectives; (3) Individual Improvement Guides.

There are seven steps for developing the School/Department Improvement Plan: Step I—Identify the area for improvement; Step II—Outline the problem; Step III—Develop performance objectives; Step IV—Construct step-by-step breakdown of action required; Step V—Indicate target dates; Step VI—Identify the person responsible for achieving each step of the action plan; Step VII—Review performance.

There are six steps for constructing the Individual Improvement Plan: Step I—Identify key results area; Step II—Cite the improvement action; Step III—Develop step-by-step breakdown of action required; Step IV—Devise target dates; Step V—Identify individual responsibility; Step VI—Summarize the performance outcome.

INDIVIDUAL IMPROVEMENT PLAN

Dr. John Wilkenson
ADMINISTRATOR / SUPERVISOR

High School Principal
POSITION

October 1, 19--
DATE

GODARD PUBLIC SCHOOLS

HAVEN, NEW YORK

EXHIBIT 10-2

Individual Improvement Plan

Date _October 1,_ 19_____

Key Area	Improvement Action (Objectives)	Step-by-Step Breakdown of Action Required
Organization	To become knowledgable about the concept of School Management by Objectives by: a. Reading two appropriate books on the subject b. Attending two workshops c. Discussing the concept with noted personages who are familiar with the concept d. Visiting two schools which have successfully implemented the concept, to be performed by June 30, 19--	1. Read the following books on management by objectives: a. John W. Humble, _Management Objectives in Action_, McGraw-Hill, London, 1970. b. Dale D. McConkey, _How to Manage by Results_, American Management Association, New York, 1965. c. J.D. Batten, _Beyond Manage by Objectives_, American Management Association, New York, 1966. 2. Attend Conference sponsored by A.M.A. entitled "Installing Management by Objectives." 3. Attend workshop given by SMBO advisor. 4. Visit the following school districts which have implemented and discuss concept with administrators and supervisors; obtain written materials and forms used by the respective school districts which have implemented SMBO and discuss concept a. Trenton Public Schools b. Winnetka Public Schools c. Westport Public Schools Westport, Connecticut 5. Develop procedural plan for installing SMBO in high school. 6. Spend two days in Massachusetts discussing our plan for implementing SMBO with professors from Harvard University and MIT.

EXHIBIT 10-2 (continued)

Administrator/Supervisor __Dr. John Wilkenson__

Position __High School Principal__

Target Date	By Whom	Outcome: (Results, delays, amendments)
October 15, 19--	High school principal	On plan -- All three books were informative and comprehensive; however I found J.D. Batten's book invaluable because it covered the human aspects of SMBO.
November 7-9, 19--	High school principal	On plan -- Very professional-like, informative conference. Many state and governmental agencies were represented.
Weekend of November 13, 19--	High school principal, assistant principal, and all department chairman	
December 4, 19--	High school principal	On plan --
December 11, 19--	High school principal	On plan --
December 18, 19--	High school principal	On plan --
January 10, 19--	SMBO advisor, high school principal, assistant principal & dept. chairman	Above plan -- First draft of procedural plan was completed on January 5, 19--
January 15, 19--	SMBO advisor and high school principal	On plan -- The visit to Harvard University and MIT proved to be highly informative and many suggestions were offered for improving our plan.

EXHIBIT 10-2 (continued)

Individual Improvement Plan

Date <u>October 1,</u> 19 _____

Key Area	Improvement Action (Objectives)	Step-by-Step Breakdown of Action Required
		7. Discuss trip to Harvard University and MIT with department chairman
		8. Incorporate suggestions as modified by the department chairman in procedural plan; distribute draft to all administrators and supervisors in high school.

EXHIBIT 10-2 (continued)

Administrator/Supervisor <u>Dr. John Wilkenson</u>

Position <u>High School Principal</u>

Target Date	By Whom	Outcome: (Results, delays, amendments)
February 1, 19--	SMBO advisor, high school principal and representative from the department chairman	On Plan - Discussion with the dept. chairman continued for 3 1/2 hours.
February 15, 19--	High school principal	On Plan - Procedural plan completed and distributed to administrators and supervisors; copies also to library.

EXHIBIT 10-2 (continued)

ELEVEN

Training an Advisor for Implementing School MBO

The improvement process of a complex organization such as a school system is an important matter and cannot be left to mere chance. School districts which have implemented School MBO have not been able to get maximum results for a number of reasons, chief among which is the absence of an administrator who has full charge for the implementation of the program. The term "School MBO advisor" is used to identify the administrator concerned with advising educators in the implementation of School Management by Objectives. It is possible to implement this concept without such a person; however, without training and assistance from an "expert," each administrator and supervisor will find it difficult to develop high quality analysis. It will also take much longer to learn to operate within the framework of the School MBO program because the administrators and supervisors will have to learn by trial and error what can be more easily acquired through the instruction and training of an advisor. If too much time is consumed in getting the program operating, the educators will lose some of the benefits which only occur when the primary analysis and implementation details have been accomplished. The advisor also plays a role as a "change agent" within the school district. To attempt to implement without a knowledgeable authority is foolhardy; indeed, one might say that attempting the program without employing a management authority to oversee its operation would almost inevitably doom the program to failure. The School MBO advisor can play an important role in helping each individual administrator and supervisor to approach his job analysis in a less introspective manner; he also provides an outside force in generating ideas for improved performance. The intent of this chapter is to identify the need for a School MBO advisor, to cite the conditions existing in a school which necessitate the employment of such a position, to define the role of the advisor, to state the qualifications for the position and to highlight the training role of the advisor.

IDENTIFYING THE THREE MAIN PROCESSES TO SCHOOL MBO

There are three main processes to an effective School MBO program.

First, the philosophy of the school district is defined in terms of educational objectives and long-range goals. This framework enables the main criteria of successful performance to be identified.

Second, all administrators and supervisors are required to identify the individual contribution they make towards the achievement of the school's goals and objectives. This is accomplished through the guides and improvement plans.

Third, the major and perhaps the most important process of a School MBO program is the process of periodic reviews of performance between the educator and his immediate supervisors.

There are several situations in which these performance reviews are especially valuable:

School District

- When a school district has maintained its status quo for many years and needs something to stimulate growth and possibly develop innovative procedures to jar complacency in the school and the community.
- When a school district is moving in an exploratory direction, attempting new methods and innovative programs, and has a goal of educational improvement that will provide students with maximum educational benefits.
- When an ineffectual performance appraisal program is being enforced.
- When operations have been based on expediency and the need for long-range planning is obvious.

Staff

- When a group wants and needs help in defining and limiting a problem.
- When staff members have run out of ideas.
- When there is a need for progress evaluation.
- When staff need special or technical information.
- When staff have become lethargic and need some kind of rejuvenation.
- When staff need summing up and assessing the work they have already done.

- When staff need help in determining the next step to follow.
- When there is a need to establish better communication between the chief school officer and staff.
- When a school needs to establish, conduct and evaluate training improvement programs.

Individuals

- When an educator's incompetence is apparent.
- When an administrator or supervisor is not certain as to his exact role and responsibility.
- When initiating an individual accountability program.
- Where there is a need to design more effective training programs for meeting the needs of individual staff members.

DEFINING THE ROLE OF THE SCHOOL MBO ADVISOR

The advisor has the responsibility of assisting administrators and supervisors to improve school performance through a systematic improvement program. Given this charge, he performs the following functions:

1. Assists chief school officer in launching and implementing school improvement program.

The advisor helps the chief school officer develop a commitment to the program and assess strategy for its successful implementation. He also assists in developing district-wide objectives and the overall plan. He establishes the timetable to install School MBO and all policies, procedures and guidelines to ensure the success of the program. He also plans, develops and maintains a resource area for storing forms, materials and books that will be of assistance to administrators and supervisors.

2. Meets with individuals, small groups, departments, and schools to explain and delineate the School MBO program.

The School MBO plan cannot succeed without the complete understanding and cooperation of the faculty members. Therefore, it is imperative that the advisor establish seminars with administrators and faculty members in order to orient them to the full scope, methods, and objectives of the School MBO plan. Once the program has been set in motion, the advisor must work with the faculty as closely as possible. In this capacity he must constantly advise and coordinate the efforts of all the groups involved. This should be done by working with individuals and groups within the school system when necessary.

3. Assists administrators and supervisors in developing key results analysis and improvement plans.

This is the most difficult and all-important task in that it is directly concerned with success or failure of the job as a whole. The advisor must see to it that each key result area is reasonably independent and assessable, covering all major job functions, and in line with school goals and objectives. He must be adept in classifying criteria of performance into key results areas. He must be able to help administrators and supervisors draft their improvement guides and plans. Eventually the administrators and supervisors will be able to complete their own guides and plans without the aid of the advisor.

4. Subsequently, assists administrators and supervisors in analyzing problem areas for developing performance improvement programs.

The advisor should also carefully analyze all variances in outcome on plans at all levels. He would look for relationships between "delays," "amendments," and "below-plan results" to determine the extent to which they might reflect larger problems. This advisor would also make it possible for him to aid in developing suggestions for improvement for individual administrators as well as for departments and schools. (Because of his broader base of knowledge regarding problems facing the school district, he would be better able to determine what needs to be done to achieve higher performance standards as well as who needs to do it.)

5. Assists administrators and supervisors in identifying problems that emerge as a result of performance review.

The advisor must set up procedures for systematically reviewing performance, determining which are *above*, *on* or *below* plan. In performing this duty he must be highly visual, i.e., he must visit, confer frequently with his staff and in general make sure the School/Department Improvement Plan is a working reality and not just a "paper plan." It is possible that outcomes that are above (or even on) plan are the results of objectives that were too low; in such cases the advisor could re-evaluate these objectives.

Objectives that are below plan must be recognized by the advisor and followed up. In this case he would meet with the involved staff member(s) and assist them in either revising, modifying, deleting or adding new action plans or possibly new objectives. Correcting below-plan outcomes must be one of the items of greatest priority.

The advisor must also be alert to emerging patterns in particular areas if improvement is to be effected. From his vantage point, he must be able to pinpoint problems that are perhaps too close to the administrators and supervisors for them to identify.

6. Conducts analysis of training needs and initiates training programs.

The advisor must be able to assess the need for a training development program; create such a program; be involved in the administration of the program; evaluate the total training program.

Since the task of the advisor is to improve the performance of administrators and supervisors, he must decide where the improvement is needed, how much improvement should be provided, and for whom. Once this has been accomplished, the advisor, assisted by the personnel administrator, should establish the training program or programs that fit the needs of the staff. The next step for the advisor is to handle the task of bringing about the improvement itself. Here the advisor may conduct a training development program, help others to teach it, or advise on the program approaches and developments. Finally, the advisor, to be even more effective in bringing about that desirable change, should check on the actions of administrators and supervisors after the training development program has been concluded. The "check" would enable the advisor to determine whether the training programs were successful or whether further training is necessary.

7. Has the responsibility for monitoring the school improvement program to prevent problems usually associated with the initial implementation stage and to correct problems should they occur.

The advisor must monitor improvement plans for individual administrators, departments, and schools, to guard against confused descriptions, imprecise statements of objectives, inordinate degrees of attention and energy being expended upon trivial problems, inadequate controls, failures to raise the levels of performance expectations from year to year, unrealistic statements of objectives, and conflict between the objectives determined by various individuals, departments, or schools with respect to each other and *vis à vis* the long-term goals of the district as a whole.

8. Assists school officials, administrators, teachers, students and community members to conduct needs assessment program in order to reveal strengths and weaknesses of school district.

Ever since the Sputnik crisis of the 1950's, public education has been faced with persistent calls for "progress." However, in order to move forward, to progress, a school system must first be well aware of its current standing. In other words, if it doesn't know "where it is," how can it know "where it wants to go" for the future? In order to assess the present situation, school districts need evaluative data, but most school personnel (from top level administrators to individual classroom teachers) are not trained to recognize relevant data or to systematically gather it for analysis. The advisor would help train personnel in data collection and would conduct the analysis necessary to make this data useful.

9. Counsels administrators and supervisors who are experiencing difficulty with implementation of the program, and consequently acts as the ultimate authority in the implementation of the program.

The advisor *must be the ultimate authority* in the functioning of the School MBO program. He must be readily available to counsel and coach and make decisions when difficulties arise. He must be centrally located, yet free to meet in problem-solving situations in an attempt to bring group efforts together to improve performance.

10. Assists the chief school officer in diagnosing areas in which the system's effectiveness is weak.

Some areas that come to mind are: improper delegation of responsibility and authority; objectives of departments or various administrators not in line with school objectives; confusion between administrative and supervisory jobs; too many levels in the organizational structure; missing function.

QUALIFICATIONS FOR THE POSITION OF A SCHOOL MBO ADVISOR

Improving school performance is no ordinary job. Many school districts have set out on a course for improving performance and have failed. The job will necessitate an educator with a great deal of drive, motivation, creativity and insight. The following is a brief description of the special qualifications of the School MBO advisor.

Academic Preparation

The advisor should have a four-year B.A. or B.S. degree in liberal arts, preferably with a major either in psychology, English, business or sociology. He should have an M.A. or M.S. degree in education with emphasis in elementary and secondary education. He should have either a Ph.D. or an Ed.D. in supervision, educational administration, or management.

Experience

The advisor should have five years of teaching experience in public elementary and secondary schools. He should have a minimum of two years of experience in supervision and four years of administrative experience as an elementary or secondary principal. A minimum of two years of experience on the central administration level is also desirable.

Special Features

The person chosen for the position should be well trained and extremely knowledgeable in the School MBO concept: its techniques, its implementation and its pitfalls. Although a district might designate someone within the administrative team to oversee the program, the position must be an independent one; that is, the advisor must have no other responsibility or duty other than overseeing and implementing the program. He must have free rein, be accountable solely to the chief school officer, and be accessible at all times to personnel in the district. The advisor cannot have a part-time position; there must be a trained authority available constantly for trouble-shooting, analysis, diagnosis and counseling if the improvement program is to succeed. Obviously, the advisor cannot have shared responsibilities or obligations.

Important Job Skills

The advisor must possess a number of important job skills in order to initiate, implement, and follow though a School MBO program. Some of these skills are cited below:

1. *Organization and efficiency*: The advisor must have the ability to coordinate and supervise programs. He must be able to establish a comprehensive operational structure in order to successfully implement the program. He must have the ability to manage and oversee all programs in order to ensure their efficient operation.
2. *Ability to work with basic understandings*: The advisor must be able to recognize basic conceptual problems in order to successfully manipulate the programs so as to operate a productive plan. He must have the ability to foresee and understand all situations that could arise during the implementation of School MBO.

3. *Understanding of the operation of a school system*: It is essential for an advisor to be cognizant of the many and complex roles involved in the operation of a school district. This is important in order for him to successfully relate to the administrators and faculty members and their respective obligations and duties in the School MBO program.
4. *Ability to work with people*: The advisor must be able to communicate and work with other people in order to generate enthusiasm for the plan in the community as well as within the school district. He must be aware of the social composition and problems of the community in order to implement a productive program within the limits of the social environment.
5. *Trouble-shooter*: A function of the advisor is to be aware of all snags that may develop. In essence he must be a trouble-shooter. In this capacity, he either prevents problems before they develop or solves those that develop as soon as possible.
6. *Conceptual skills*: The advisor must have a "larger" view, in order to be able to help those of shorter or narrower vision to understand the implications of the broader view for their individual tasks.
7. *Professional knowledge and skills*: It is the duty of the advisor to utilize his years of experience in the operation of schools and methods of teaching when making decisions, solving problems and resolving problems that arise in the program. The "crisis in education" is due in part to the fact that educators are not making proper use of professional know-how in meeting present-day problems.
8. *Community consultant*: The advisor must work not only within the school system but also within the community. This can be done by working with key individuals in the community, and by releasing publications informing the public of the purpose, methods, and goals of the program.

It might help to identify what the role of the School MBO advisor is *not*:

1. He is not a consultant and usually does not make recommendations; however, he is a representative of the chief school officer.
2. He is not a diagnostician per se, but should activate discussion for problem-solving.
3. He does not substitute for either administrators or supervisors.

In the final analysis, the advisor's primary role is that of coaching and training administrators and supervisors in a continuous cycle for improving school performance. His job is analogous to the systems analyst in the computer industry. He is the one who sees the complete picture and is able to coordinate, integrate and fit into the whole scheme the job responsibilities of all personnel. With his guidance the sum of all the parts must yield a total system which meets the objectives of the school system.

THE ROLE OF SCHOOL MBO ADVISOR: A TRAINING FUNCTION

The training of educators for installing a School MBO program is the responsibility of the advisor. The course material should be developed by the advisor to suit the particular needs of the school district. The author doubts seriously whether external training courses would be of much help when installing the program for the first time. At any rate, internal orientation mini-courses would have to be given in order to get the program operating smoothly.

TRAINING EDUCATORS TO IMPLEMENT A SCHOOL MBO PROGRAM

The training of educators to improve performance consists of a number of seminars concentrating on specific areas and taken in sequence. The format for each day of the seminar involves two basic phases: Phase One—technical information and explanation; Phase Two—application of knowledge gained in Phase One. The latter portion of this training course evolves in a number of workshops which include role playing and other forms of interaction training methods.

The following is an outline of a seminar used by the author to train educators to implement School MBO:

SCHOOL MANAGEMENT BY OBJECTIVES SEMINAR

I. Preparation for Seminar (one week before seminar)
1. Study "Guide for Installing Management by Objectives in Education."
2. Develop over head transparencies for seminar.
3. Check to determine if improvement guides and plans are available for each participant enrolled in the seminar.
4. Prepare three case studies to discuss during the seminar.
II. First Day
1. Introduction
   a) define Management by Objectives
   b) identify its essential features
   c) delineate the importance of MBO
   d) state the problems associated with MBO
   e) identify the steps in installing MBO in education

2. Conducting a Critical Analysis
   a) delineate the steps for conducting a critical analysis
   b) identify some major key areas
   c) state the sources where information can be obtained
3. Workshop: Participants will break down a major key area into components and develop a critical analysis

III. Second Day

1. Constructing or Rewriting the Job Description
   a) define a job description
   b) identify its essential components
   c) state the process of writing the job description
   d) delineate the significant characteristic of the job description
   e) identify the major administrative job functions
2. Workshop: Participants will write a correctly written job description realizing its working relationship, its broad function and principal areas of responsibilities
3. Developing a Key Results Analysis (Constructing Individual Improvement Guide)
   a) define key results analysis
   b) identify the components of Individual Improvement Guide
   c) describe key result areas
   d) define performance standards
   e) identify basic characteristic of performance standards
   f) describe methods of checking performance
   g) identify suggestions for improving performance
   h) describe the process of mutually agreeing on Individual Improvement Guide

IV. Third Day

Workshop: Participants will conduct a key results analysis which will include the following activities:
   a) match description of key areas with performance standards
   b) write methods of checking performance
   c) match performance standards with methods of checking performance
   d) devise suggestions for improving performance
   e) reach a mutual agreement on Individual Improvement guide
1. Constructing Improvement Plans
   a) outline a problem
   b) identify the procedures for determining the most appropriate solution to a problem

    c) define long-range goals and short-range objectives

    d) state the purposes of long-range goals and short-range objectives

    e) delineate the guidelines for developing long-range goals

    f) define an action plan

    g) identify factors affecting the constructing of action plan

    h) state the procedural steps for constructing an action plan

    i) identify the procedural steps for reviewing performances

    j) describe the process of mutually agreeing on School/ Department Improving Plan and Individual Improvement Plan

V.   Fourth and Fifth Day

Workshop: Participants will complete a School/Department Improvement Plan and Individual Improvement Plan which will include the following activities:

    a) cite a problem

    b) state key areas and problems

    c) make proper use of problem-solving guide

    d) write a long-range goal

    e) develop performance objectives

    f) relate long-range goals to short-range objectives

    g) construct short-range objectives and action plans

    h) demonstrate the correct procedure for reaching a mutual agreement on School/Department Improving Plan and Individual Improvement Plan

Summary and Conclusion

    a) techniques for obtaining improved performance

    b) case studies of three school districts which have implemented MBO

    c) the future of School MBO

SUMMARY

The improvement process of a school district is an important process and cannot be left to chance. The need for a person such as an advisor to be in charge of the School MBO program, should be obvious.

The three main processes to an effective School MBO program are: First, the philosophy of the school district is defined in terms of educational and long-range goals; second, all administrators and supervisors are required to identify their individual contributions toward school goals attainment; third, the process is of major importance and it is this process which provides the basis for the establishment of a position of School MBO advisor.

The role of the advisor is to: (1) assist in the definition of key areas and tasks; (2) help administrators and supervisors draft their individual guides and plans; (3) assist in the negotiation process; (4) assist in conducting problem-solving conferences; (5) establish a timetable for installing the School MBO program. The School MBO advisor is not: (1) a consultant; (2) a diagnostician; (3) a substitute administrator or supervisor. The primary role of the advisor is that of training for improving school performance.

The training program for School MBO involves two basic phases: Phase One—technical information and explanation; Phase Two—application of knowledge gained in Phase One. The latter portion of this training course evolves in a number of workshops which include role-playing and other forms of interaction training methods.

TWELVE

Formulating the Training Program

School MBO is by its very nature an effective approach to the objective evaluation measurement and improvement of educators' performances. It is readily apparent that the process of analyzing and meeting the training needs of teachers, supervisors and administrators is already built into the approach. The concept can succeed only when it is an accepted way of operating a school district. Effective administrative and supervising development and training are important by-products. School personnel development and training are not new—in one way or another their by-products have been with the school district for years. What is new is the way the training needs are analyzed and met through the process of School MBO. Most educators would probably agree with the author when he states that ". . . it is high time for administrators to remove from the educational scene the traditional way of determining training and development needs and to give way to a new approach which not only systematically, analytically and objectively determines training and development needs of educators, but evaluates the effectiveness of the total training program. I am referring, of course, to the concept of School MBO."[1] This chapter will identify the relationship between School MBO and the training program, cite the training process of School MBO, explain how to establish broad and specific training needs, and state the benefits to be derived from training programs keyed to School MBO.

---

[1] From a speech delivered to chief school officers at a conference held by the National Alliance of Black School Superintendents in New Orleans, Louisiana, November 16-18, 1973.

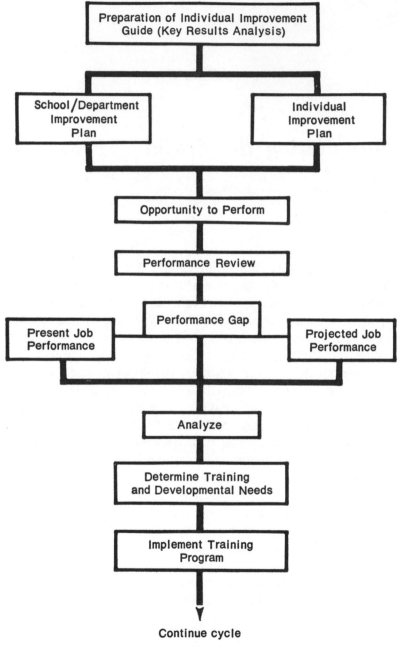

FIGURE 12-1
The Relationship Between School MBO and the Training Program

IDENTIFYING THE RELATIONSHIP BETWEEN SCHOOL MBO AND THE TRAINING PROGRAM

Figure 12-1 illustrates how School MBO can aid the school district in identifying training needs and demonstrates how the process is closely tied to the training program. The preparation of the Individual Improvement Guide helps to determine the required level of performance. After the Guide is completed and mutually agreed to by the parties involved, problems are determined and objectives and action plans are developed to solve the cited problems. Actions for solving the problems are recorded in the School/Department Improvement Plan and the Individual Improvement Plan. Effort is exerted to achieve the objectives. Actual or present job performance is measured against projected job performance. The difference determines the performance gap, which sets the basis for the training program. Training plans are developed for improving performance. The training program is implemented. The training program is evaluated to determine if it brought about the necessary improvement in performance. The cycle is repeated.

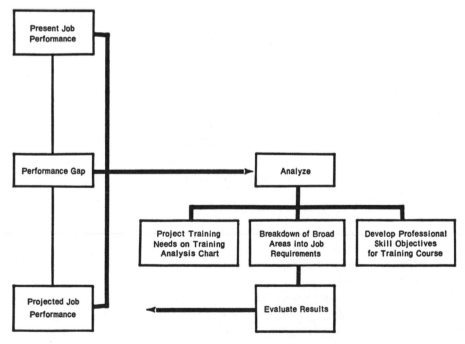

FIGURE 12-2
The Training Process of School Management by Objectives

THE TRAINING PROCESS OF SCHOOL MBO

The training process of School MBO is illustrated in Figure 12-2. Present job performance is measured against projected job performance (performance objectives and action plans). The performance gap is determined and analyzed. The broad training needs are projected on a Training Analysis Chart. The training needs are further broken down into specific job requirements. Professional skill objectives are devised for each specific job requirement. The results of the training program are measured against projected job performance.

ESTABLISHING BROAD AND SPECIFIC TRAINING NEEDS

The results of performance appraisal review of each administrator are used as the basis for determining broad training needs. At times, the immediate supervisor may make recommendations in terms of specific areas in which he thinks his staff may need some training. In the left column of the Training Analysis Chart shown in Figure 12-3, the name of each administrator who is being considered for training is indicated. The broad training areas are indicated at the top of the chart. Each administrator training need is analyzed in terms of each specified training area. Those areas needing improvement are marked with an "X." When each administrator's training needs have been identified and checked off, the resultant chart displays the individual training deficiencies of all administrators listed on the chart.

After the Training Analysis Chart has been completed and analyzed, a further breakdown is warranted for determining specific training needs. An analysis of the broad training needs would reveal that "writing performance objectives" is the area shown on the chart which needs top priority because more administrators are weaker in this one particular area than in any other. Figure 12-4 illustrates how this broad area is broken down into specific training needs. The left column contains the broad training need area. The middle column contains a detailed breakdown of the needs in the job situation. Each specific need is illustrated. The right column contains an objective which is keyed to each job situation need. The resultant effort is a specific training guide or curriculum for the training program. All broad training needs are broken down in this manner.

When this stage has been completed, it is possible to identify an individual deficiency by completing and analyzing a chart similar to the one indicated in Figure 12-5. This chart relates to the specific job requirements that are necessary to achieve projected job performance. When this chart has been completed

Personnel to be Trained	Coaching & Counseling	Writing Performance Objective	Public Relations	Effective Communication	Report Writing	Leadership Skills	Monitoring Teacher Performance	Performance Appraisal	Staff Participation	Long–range Planning	Problem Solving	Program Implementation
James B.	X	X								X		X
Joseph K.		X	X		X	X	X		X		X	
Arthur F.		X	X				X			X	X	
James H.	X		X	X		X		X	X		X	X
Doris W.	X		X			X	X			X		X
Barbara G.	X	X						X	X			
George R.		X		X			X		X	X		X
George C.		X	X		X			X	X			X
Donald R.										X		
Anthony M.		X					X				X	X
Cheryl G.		X			X				X			
Donald H.		X		X					X		X	

FIGURE 12-3
Training Analysis Chart

Training Method: Broad Area	Detailed Need in Job Situation	Professional Skill Objectives
1. Writing performance objectives	1.1 Understanding the importance of writing correctly stated performance objectives, performance standards and action plans	to explain the reason for writing performance objectives
	1.2 Understanding the interlocking relationship between long-range goals and short-range objectives	to illustrate the relationship between long-range goals and short-range objectives
	1.3 Technique to writing long-range goals	to construct long-range goals
	1.4 Technique to writing correctly stated performance objectives	to develop short-range objectives
	1.5 Understanding constraints on objectives	to derive performance standards for objectives
	1.6 Knowledgeable in step-by-step breaking down in achieving objective	to develop an action plan for achieving an objective

FIGURE 12-4
Example of Breakdown of Broad Areas in Job Requirement

Personnel to be Trained	Explore reasons for writing performance objectives	Illustrate relationship be-tween long—range goals & short—range objectives	Construct long—range goals	Develop short—range objectives	Device performance standards	Develop action plans
James B.	X		X	X	X	X
Joseph K.	X	X	X			X
Arthur F.	X		X		X	X
James H.	X	X	X	X	X	X
Doris W.	X	X	X		X	
Barbara G.	X	X	X	X	X	X
George R.	X					
George C.	X	X	X	X		X
Donald K.	X					
Anthony M	X	X	X	X	X	
Cheryl C.	X					
Donald H.	X			X	X	X

FIGURE 12-5
Specific Requirements for Conducting the Training Course

and analyzed it serves as the basis for conducting the training course for the specific training deficiency. A chart should be constructed for each training deficiency to meet the projected job performance requirements. The chart is developed jointly by the administrator in charge of personnel training and development, the School MBO advisor and the supervisors. Preparations are made to implement the training course.

BENEFITS TO BE DERIVED FROM TRAINING PROGRAM

The following are some advantages of the training and developmental program emanating from the adoption of School MBO:

1. Training becomes increasingly focused on what the *administrator* is required to achieve rather than on what he should know.
2. Because of the close involvement of *educator* and *supervisor* in the process of analyzing and meeting training needs, *administrators* approach their training experiences positively, and derive more benefit.
3. One can evaluate more objectively the results of training in terms of improved job performance.
4. A better analytical tool for identifying knowledge, skill, and attitudes required for individual posts evolves; this tool is useful in selection of personnel.
5. As future demands are anticipated, it is possible to identify and subsequently develop *administrators* with potential more objectively.
6. More constructive career guidance can be offered to individual *administrators* because of the clearer picture there is of individual job positions throughout the *administrative* structure.[2]

SUMMARY

The procedural steps for analyzing and meeting the training needs of administrators are as follows: (1) Use the performance review as the basis for determining the performance gap; (2) Project broad training needs on Training Analysis Chart; (3) Break down broad areas into job requirements; (4) Develop professional skill objectives for implementing training course; (5) Measure effectiveness of training program against projected job performance.

---

[2]John W. Humble, *Management by Objectives in Action*; J. H. Binnie, *Analyzing and Meeting the Training Needs of Management*, McGraw-Hill: London, England, 1970, pp. 245-246. The author has substituted the term "manager" for "administrator": "educator and supervisor" for "man and boss" and "administrative" for "management" from the original text of J. H. Binnie.

THIRTEEN

Reaching Beyond School Management by Objectives

The school district which is committed to excellence must do more than establish goals, set objectives and devise action plans. The main ingredient of the system, the human being, without which there would be no school system, must be integrated with other resources such as materials, money, time, equipment and space. It was Batten who stated, "Individualism is vital, but a combination of individuals will be only a group of individuals—not an organization—unless the requirements for successful operation are skillfully blended."[1] Unless an effort is made to the contrary, School MBO in itself will not guarantee improved performance. In fact it can be a source for nurturing mediocrity simply because some administrators and supervisors are satisfied to sit back and let things happen.

School MBO will demand a great deal of hard work beyond the stages of implementation, involvement, conviction and commitment. In fact, developing the Individual Improvement Guide, School/Department Improvement Plans and Individual Improvement Plan is, at most, about 30 per cent of the job. Batten maintains, "It is only the bones, the skeleton of the school body. The problem is to move out beyond Management by Objectives and begin the process of making the organization operative through a planned motivational climate."

The rationale for this chapter is to focus on an understanding of motivation, identify the role of perception in motivation, discuss the prerequisites of motivation, list motivational needs and delineate school enrichment opportunities for enhancing the motivational climate for improving individual and collective results.

---

[1]J. P. Batten, "Beyond Management by Objectives," American Management Association, New York, N.Y., 1966, pp. 9-10.

UNDERSTANDING MOTIVATION

Motivating educators deals not only with the problem of stimulating them to perform effectively; it also deals with the removal of conditions which make them dissatisfied with their job. When educators believe in and understand what needs to be accomplished, when they are stimulated to use their skills and abilities to perform what they are really interested in, then and only then will they perform effectively. Administrators and supervisors therefore must understand that the most effective way to get an educator to perform effectively is to make him *want* to do it.

Each educator has his own zone of acceptance. Performance requirements falling within this zone will be achieved with a minimum of problems. However, performance requirements which fall outside of this zone will be achieved carelessly or dishonestly, or may even be sabotaged. The real role of the administrator or supervisor is to enlarge this "outside" zone. The task of enlarging educators' acceptance to perform well is reaching beyond School MBO.

THE ROLE OF PERCEPTION IN MOTIVATION

Every administrator and supervisor must understand that teachers' personal goals play a dominant role in their motivation. When a teacher is deciding to take a particular course of action, he unconsciously examines it to determine whether or not it will fulfill his own personal goals as well as those of the school system. Hughes holds that:

> Insensitive administrators fail to perceive people as having personal needs and goals because they do not understand their own needs and goals. They cannot possibly tap the human potentialities of people at work. Using, as they do, restrictions, threats of punishment, and psychological distance to control employees' behavior, they cannot help but increase feelings of guilt and hostility toward management which result in interpersonal conflict.[2]

Any person who feels that educators should be interested solely in achieving the goals of the school system is unaware of the nature of human beings. There is absolutely nothing wrong, unethical or unprofessional in an educator's working to fulfill his personal goals. It is the responsibility of the administrator or supervisor to integrate personal goals with school goals.

---

[2]Charles L. Hughes, "Goal-setting Key to Individual and Organizational Effectiveness," American Management Association, New York, N.Y., 1965, p. 59.

Educators set personal goals because of five basic needs. When these needs are met they set the stage for motivation.

IDENTIFYING THE PREREQUISITES FOR MOTIVATION

All educators need to be maintained, just as buildings and machines must be maintained. The maintenance needs of teachers, supervisors, and administrators are quite similar to those of other people such as lawyers, doctors, presidents of companies, bus drivers, teacher's aides or, for that matter, the President of the United States. Motivation and maintenance needs have distinctively separate characteristics and effects on educators in school.[3] Behavorial theorists maintain that lower order (maintenance) needs must be fairly well satisfied before higher level (motivation) needs emerge.[4] Both types of needs must be met. Neither set will supplement the other. Hughes states, "Maintenance needs avoid dissatisfaction through the environment. Motivation needs are satisfied through achievement of personal goals."[5]

Maintenance needs are in areas of economic security, orientation, status, social and physical factors.

Economic maintenance needs for the educator involve salary and fringe benefits. Economic maintenance needs do not include awards for meritorious service; merit pay is usually a reinforcement of motivation.

Security maintenance needs refer to an educator's feeling which emanates primarily from his perception of his supervisor as a democratic leader and a congenial person and from the knowledge that he is protected by a non-threatening school environment.

Orientation maintenance needs refer to the educator's familiarity with the school system and the place of his assignment in the system. This information should be supplied at the annual teacher orientation meeting in September, with the teachers' handbook and other pertinent literature. Teachers should also be confident that their information will be kept up to date by frequent bulletins.

Status maintenance needs are usually satisfied through job classifications, title, furnishings, privileges, relationships and the school's image. The process of job promotion is usually related to motivational factors; however, the status is basically a maintenance factor.

Social maintenance needs are satisfied through formal and informal group meetings, conferences and after-school recreational activities.

---

[3]M. Scott Myers, "Who Are Your Motivated Workers?" *Harvard Business Review*, January-February, 1964.

[4]A. H. Maslow, *Motivation and Personality*, Harper Brothers, 1954.

[5]Hughes, *loc. cit.*, p. 34.

Physical maintenance needs are primarily satisfied through the organization of the job or the physical environment where the performance will take place, such as parking facilities, heating, air conditioning, lighting, rest rooms, teachers' lounge, noise level, etc.[6]

When these maintenance needs are adequately satisfied, they minimize job dissatisfaction and set the stage for creating a desirable motivational climate.

Item:

A school district located in the South uses School MBO primarily for establishing an accountability program and improving performance. The system was limited to principals. Performance objectives are set for a one-year period and performance is reviewed semi-annually. All principals are required to set four objectives for their respective schools which are mutually agreed to by their supervisors. When the objectives are finally agreed to, the principals each receive $500. Each principal can receive up to $2500 depending upon the weight of the objectives and performance results. The program was moderately successful. This was primarily because the bonus was substituted for the annual increment. In essence, there was no additive incentive for achieving. An annual increment becomes a part of an educator's maintenance needs. Maintenance needs do not motivate performance but are a prerequisite for motivation. When a bonus was substituted for an annual increment, the principals were not really motivated to perform. The performance which was achieved is most likely that which would have been accomplished if the principals had enjoyed the annual increment. An effective plan which is designed to motivate performance must also include those items which are a part of the maintenance needs of the educator; that is, the annual increment should have continued, and the bonus added as an incentive for improved performance.

DEFINING MOTIVATIONAL NEEDS

When motivation needs are met, effective performances in the school system can be expected. Once an educator is committed to school organizational goals, his potential is tremendous provided that simultaneously his personal goals are integrated with those of the school.

Educators have such motivational needs as professional growth, visible achievement, recognized responsibility and tangible recognition.

Growth refers to mental growth. Mental growth in the realm of education would involve: (1) keeping up with new techniques and methods; (2) improv-

---

[6]M. Scott Myers, *Every Employee a Manager*, McGraw-Hill Book Company, New York, N.Y., 1970, pp. 11-12.

ing teaching or administrative competence; (3) adapting to changing practices and values; (4) maintaining physical fitness; (5) overcoming inflexibility. One of the most important methods of motivating through mental growth is through an innovative school system which consistently provides challenging situations for the professional staff.

Achievement refers to the need for achievement by educators. Teachers and administrators differ in terms of their need for achievement. A teacher or administrator's level of motivation will vary with his opportunity to find expression for it. In a rigidly traditional school system, there may be very little opportunity for achievement; therefore, the school will most likely attract low-achieving people. An innovative school system with a reputation for doing some exciting things would most likely be attractive for high-achieving educators. School systems that attract low-achieving educators are usually satisfied primarily through the maintenance factors.

Responsibility refers to a sense of commitment to performing well in the school system. Administrators tend to have a higher sense of responsibility for performing than teachers do. This is primarily because a sense of responsibility is a function of level in the organization. The superintendent assumes more responsibility than the classroom teacher. In fact, salaries are predicated on the amount of responsibility which comes with the position. However, it is also true that motivation through responsibility can be brought about by the leadership style of the administrator. An administrator whose style of leadership is primarily autocratic will restrict the extent to which educators assume responsibilities for various tasks. On the other hand, the administrator who practices the participatory decision-making process by involving his staff in the affairs that affect them will most likely motivate staff to assume added responsibility in terms of job achievements.

Recognition refers to the recognition an educator earns from outstanding service. Recognition as a positive feedback is a reinforcement for motivating educators for improving performance. Recognition is at its highest point in motivating behavior when it comes from the person himself. For example, when a third grade teacher increased the number of students reading on a grade level in her class from four to 22, the progression of successes recognized by the teacher was the primary motivating factor. Scott Myers states, "Ideally, recognition should not depend on an intermediary, but should be a natural expression of feedback from achievement itself."[7]

The satisfying of maintenance and motivational needs is not enough to establish the ideal motivational climate for improved performance. Creating school enrichment opportunities is the added dimension necessary to reach fully beyond School MBO.

---

[7]Ibid, p. 15.

CREATING SCHOOL ENRICHMENT OPPORTUNITIES

Simply stated, creating school enrichment opportunities refers to the process of enabling teachers to take part in the planning and control functions previously restricted to supervisors and administrators. In essence it means increasing the challenging content of the job that will cause the educator to grow both in skills and in his feeling of accomplishment. School enrichment opportunities are influenced by meaningful performance, leadership styles, meaningful goals, effective teamwork, and problem-solving goal-setting sessions.

MEANINGFUL PERFORMANCE

If educators are to perform effectively, their role cannot be confined to one of service alone. Performance must be accompanied by planning and controlling. Therefore, there are basically three phases to an educator's job regardless of his position, be it teacher, assistant teacher, supervisor or administrator: plan phase, control phase and performance stage.

The *plan phase* includes the planning and organizing functions of an educator's job, usually consisting of problem-solving, goal-setting and planning the use of resources. Planning is the main ingredient of an educator's job which gives meaning to his performance. The *performance phase* is the implementation of the plan which would include the coordination of physical and mental efforts for the achievement of goals. The *control plan* encompasses measurement, evaluation, and performance adjustment. The control plan uses the feedback process for assessing and adjusting for achievement of goals. It should be noted that it is the feedback process that gives real meaning to an educator's performance to an even greater extent than planning. Without feedback the performing educator will most likely become dissatisfied with his job. The control phase is also the basis of recycling planning, performing and controlling. Those who perform for their own satisfaction are usually engaged in meaningful goals because they are involved in the planning, performing and controlling phases of their job.

THE EFFECTS OF LEADERSHIP STYLES

The supervising style of the effective administrator or supervisor is characterized by genuine and balanced concern for the goals of the school organization and the personal goals of individual staff members. He will take time out of his busy schedule to listen to his teachers' ideas and suggestions and will attempt to see the value of their ideas even if they conflict with his own.

He will solve problems by sharing information with his teachers and by involving them not only in solving problems, but also in setting goals and objectives. He will encourage his teachers to reach out in new directions, take mistakes in stride and try diligently to discover how to avoid errors in the future. He will expect and acknowledge superior performance from his teachers. The administrator or supervisor who performs in this manner is usually identified as a democratic leader and through this leadership style he is able to create a desirable motivational climate for his school.

The autocratic leader usually has high concern for himself and the school but little concern for his staff members. He will set goals for them, leaving them without the necessary information to set their own goals. He will discourage them from deviating from specific procedures. He will expect mediocre performance and say little unless something goes wrong. He will ask for new ideas, but his mind is usually already made up. When confronted with problems or conflicts, he will attempt to suppress them or to appease the troublemaker. He will punish the educator who makes mistakes, especially those mistakes which may embarrass him.

Leadership style is obviously influenced by whether or not the leader is conscious of educators' personal goals. Usually, the democratic leader is aware that each employee of a school district has personal goals and these must be satisfied (and at any cost) if satisfactory performance is to be exerted and maintained. The autocratic leader usually ignores educators' personal goals. This accounts for the lack of effective performance in many of our schools.

The author has been requested to speak to groups of administrators on several occasions throughout the nation. At each instance, he would relate the following in order to get a response from the audience:

> I don't work for the school, I work in the school to fulfill my personal goals and as long as I support the school, I will be given the opportunity to remain in the school to fulfill my personal goals.

The responses to the above statement are usually mixed. Although no one group stated that it was unanimously in favor of this belief, one group did in fact respond completely in the opposite. The above statement is true. The poor responses displayed by administrators are an indication that many of them are not aware of their role in education.

There is a very close association between acceptance of personal goals and the attainment of educational accountability. Administrators who believe that educators have personal goals which must be satisfied are usually aware of their role as educational leaders: to integrate personal goals of educators with the organizational goals of the schools. In order to carry out this assignment, behavioral theories must be applied effectively to motivate educators to perform so that personal and organizational goals are met.

Recent trends in school organizational development are replacing autocratic orientation with a more democratic orientation to create a motivational climate for improving teacher effectiveness.

Although few educators could successfully defend autocratic leadership, this supervising style is still the most dominant form of management in our schools. True, this is partially due to habit, traditional policy, inflexible systems, insensitivity and introspective myopia. However, reaching beyond School MBO means the elimination of individual authority and the substitution of collective authority through the participatory decision-making process (democratic leadership).

MEANINGFUL GOALS

Every educator has goals. Some goals are set by the person pursuing them, some are set with the participation of other people and some are set solely by other people. Administrators and supervisors should understand that most teachers will actively strive to achieve the goals they set for themselves. When administrators or supervisors set too many goals for a teacher, he will most likely react individually or collectively to set his own goals to circumvent, modify or change their goals. These goals of avoidance and rebellion, then, become the personal goals of the teacher.

The following are factors which give meaning to goal-setting; therefore they inspire educators to achieve them. The goals which have maximum motivational value are:[8]

    1.—Influenced by the goal-setter
    2.—Visible
    3.—Desirable
    4.—Challenging
    5.—Attainable

and they lead to the satisfaction of needs for

    6.—Growth
    7.—Achievement
    8.—Responsibility
    9.—Recognition
    10.—Affiliation
    11.—Security

---

[8]M. Scott Myers, *Every Employee a Manager*, McGraw-Hill Book Company, New York, N.Y., 1970, pp. 42-43.

Improving school performance can be a motivational goal in satisfying the above condition, but only in terms of criteria meaningful to each school position. To the principal it could be position. To the principal it could be higher achievement scores on reading tests. To the teacher it could be evidence that students understand a mathematical problem. To the bus driver it could mean a safe driving record for the school year. When each of these goal-setters identifies his personal goals with improving school performance and his goals meet the criteria stated above, it can then be said that improving school performance is a meaningful goal.

EFFECTIVE TEAMWORK

Changing human behavior (motivation) should be done through the medium of teamwork rather than through individual effort. One of the primary responsibilities of administrators and supervisors is to influence behavior through active team effort. John Paul Jones has enumerated five conditions that must exist in a school in order to establish an effective motivational climate:

1. Mutual Trust—Mutual trust among educators takes a long time to build but can be destroyed in a short period of time. In a school where each educator feels free to express his optimism, can state how he feels about an issue, can ask questions which may display his misunderstanding, and can disagree with any person without concern for retaliation, ridicule, threat or any other negative consequences, there is mutual trust.
2. Mutual Support—Mutual support emanates from educators when each person has a genuine concern for his colleagues' job, welfare, growth and personal success. When mutual support is established in a school, there will be no need for individual educators to waste time and energy protecting themselves from a principal, superintendent or board member. Mutual support exists when the educators in a given school give and receive help to and from each other in accomplishing whatever activity they are working on.
3. Genuine Communication—Genuine communication exists when no educator feels he has to be concerned or guarded about what he says. This also means that the principal and supervisor don't "play games" with the staff by asking trap questions, or suggesting wrong answers to test a person's integrity.
4. Accepting Conflicts as Normal and Working Them Through —Individual educators differ uniquely from each other and will not agree on everything. A good school climate exists when each staff member accepts conflict as normal, natural and as an asset. Each educator understands that resolving conflicts is a team process and works toward that end.

5. Mutual Respect for Individual Differences—There are decisions which must be team oriented because they require the commitment of most if not all of the educators within a team or school and success cannot be achieved without this commitment. However, effective teamwork exists when individual educators are not unnecessarily asked to conform. Individual staff members should feel free to ask questions or advice from other members who, in turn, will not feel obligated to take the advice.[9]

ENGAGING EDUCATORS IN PROBLEM-SOLVING—GOAL-SETTING SESSIONS

The most effective approach to creating school enrichment opportunities is through the participatory process. An effective way to achieve this is by engaging educators in problem-solving—goal-setting sessions. The sessions are usually initiated by the supervisor when he has a problem which he cannot solve adequately or the involvement of others is required or needed. He will begin the meeting by identifying the problem to the group. At times, visual aids may be used to dramatically depict the problem; at other times another person may be invited to the conference to assist in identifying the problem. The participants at the meeting are asked to give alternative solutions to the problems. Usually, the alternatives are written on the blackboard and their implications are discussed and integrated. The role of the supervisor during the discussion is that of a conference leader. He makes no judgment about what is stated or the alternative solutions to the problems. He may and should ask thought-provoking questions to generate discussion and then synthesize ideas. The educator who attends these meetings usually will find them enjoyable, informative and stimulating, particularly if the group reaches a consensus as to the best solution to the problem and appropriate steps are taken to remedy the situation.

SUMMARY

Implementing School MBO is insufficient to substantially improve a school system. Efforts must be exerted to reach beyond this managerial process by motivating educators to perform more effectively. The motivation of educators deals not only with the problem of stimulating them to perform effectively. It also deals with the removal of conditions which make them dissatisfied with their jobs. Perception is important in understanding motivation. The prerequisites to motivation are identified as maintenance needs be-

---

[9]John Paul Jones, "The Ties That Bind," National Manufacturers, New York, 1967, pp. 27-28.

cause an educator cannot be adequately motivated unless his maintenance needs are satisfied.

Maintenance needs are defined in terms of economic security, orientation, status, social and physical factors. Motivation needs are defined in terms of growth, achievement, responsibility and recognition. Creating school enrichment opportunities enhances the motivational climate for performance improvement. Individual and collective results are influenced by leadership style, meaningful goals, effective teamwork, and problem-solving, goal-setting opportunities.

FOURTEEN

Questions and Answers on School MBO

As the author researched, theorized and hypothesized about MBO, he discussed his work with educators, businessmen, and professional people. Interestingly enough, there was considerable similarity in the questions that were raised. An attempt is made here to synthesize all of these questions, and to answer them with reference to the contents of this book.

Question: What are the key points to successful implementation of School MBO?

Answer: There are several important key points which must be kept in mind if School MBO is really going to improve the overall operations of the school system: (1) Educators must be committed to the concept and must continually demonstrate their commitment by support, endorsement and follow-through. (2) When performance objectives are settled and mutually agreed to, they must be kept alive. (3) There must be a schedule for periodic checks on performance, with the schedule scrupulously followed. (4) The fact that performance appraisal review is initiated for the purpose of improving performance, not for reprimanding and criticizing, should be reinforced. (5) Educators must view the system as a long-term and continuing way of operating the schools; the "short run" duration common with many innovations should be avoided.

Question: If the system of MBO fails to improve the school's operation, what would most likely be the probable causes?

Answer: No business firm has ever been known to discontinue MBO once it has been substantially implemented. However, it appears that the following would create some serious problems for the successful implementation of School MBO: reacting to the program as another educational gimmick rather than as a systematic approach to the successful operation of all levels within the school; poor initial planning, developing and implementing of the program; poor follow-through of the program; lack of understanding by each shool personnel of the meaning and the real value of the program; failure on the part of administrators and supervisors to properly supervise the creation of the day-to-day activities through actions rather than merely paying lip-service to the approach.

Question: Is it possible to implement School MBO in a large school district that has from 25 to 30 thousand students?

Answer: Certainly. The larger the school district the greater the need for the MBO approach. Control and coordination are difficult to maintain in large school districts, mainly because of the number of employees; however, School MBO provides a systematic approach to control and coordination through the identification of specific objectives which are mutually agreed to by educational leaders and educators. Control is maintained by the periodic review of performance and coordination is also sustained because of the dovetailing effects of this system.

Question: How far down the staff line can the system of School MBO be applied?

Answer: School MBO can and should be applied to all levels, beginning with the board of education and continuing down the staff line to the part-time bus driver.

Question: Objective-setting is not new to education; what is so significant about School MBO?

Answer: It is true that setting objectives is not new to education; however, experience has shown us that in the past most objectives were stated in general and nebulous terms. In many instances objectives were not used as general guidelines for administration, supervision and teaching in our schools. In School MBO, specific measurable objectives are determined, an action plan is developed, and target dates for achieving these objectives are set.

Question: What is the difference between behavioral objectives and performance objectives?

Answer: Essentially very little. However, the author would like to think of performance objectives as applicable to teachers, supervisors and administrators, and behavioral objectives as being directed to changing and/or modifying behavior in students.

Question: Is MBO a concept adopted by businesses some 20 or 30 years ago as a system to generate more profits? If businesses are tending to be more and more inhuman in their operations, is the concept of MBO continuing to have a dehumanizing effect on society? Why would we want to adopt this type of program?

Answer: It is true that School MBO was adopted from business and it is also true that a business firm's ultimate purpose is to generate high profits. However, over a period of years of research trial and error, it has been determined that the way to high profits coincides with respect and recognition of the dignity of the individual employee, provision for opportunity to set individual and mutually agreeable objectives. This participation of decision-making policy is one of the most human aspects of MBO, bringing with it increased dividends in terms of improved trust, better communication, better working conditions, improved staff morale and more productivity. Once educators become oriented to this process many of the ills which are presently perplexing them, such as poor control, lack of coordination, ineffective appraising program, ineffectual communication network, non-productive training of developing programs, will gradually disappear due to the systems approach of School MBO.

Question: Should the concept of School MBO be implemented on a partial basis first, e.g., in a department or school, and then be broadened out to include an entire school district?

Answer: A decision will depend on the large scope and rate of implementation of MBO and the sophistication of the school district. Some schools might wish to experiment on a small scale—for example, within a department. With proper readiness, preparation and supervision, however, the program can be successfully implemented throughout a large school district. Where the choice is to implement the program on a small scale, this author opines that it would be preferable to do so in the central administration office where top administrators and supervisors will acquire first-hand knowledge and experience with the program.

Question: Is School MBO a complicated process involving complicated and time-consuming paper work?

Answer: No, it should not be with proper administration; the paper work should only involve the Individual Improvement Guide, School/Department Improvement Plan, and Individual Improvement Plan.

Question: What are the purposes of periodic performance appraisal review sessions?

Answer: This is one means of keeping control of the activities on all operations of the schools. Periodic reviews of performance serve as interim checks on whether or not the performance of the objective is serving a useful purpose in terms of meeting the overall goals of the schools. These services also serve as communication links between the supervisor and his staff members; provide the bases upon which new objectives are set where conditions demand change; provide an excellent opportunity for coaching, counseling and appraising professional performance; and provide opportunities for setting objectives which may have mutually been set which have proven to be "off track" in the accomplishment of the objective.

Question: How are responsibility and accountability determined when the performance of an educator's objectives hinges on the performance of another educator?

Answer: There are at least three ways this particular situation, which is not uncommon, can be handled: (1) The performance objectives can be developed to cover only the specific task each has responsibility for performing. (2) If the objective is a common objective, this can be clearly stated. (3) At the performance appraisal review session it will be easy for a determination to be made as to which educator performed and which did not.

Question: Some educators who were involved in school districts which have implemented the program tend to feel that not much change was noted the first year as a result of the implementation of School MBO. What accounts for this?

Answer: Results during the first year of implementing School MBO can be expected to be relatively slight. Educators have never really had a systematic approach for operating their schools and this system will need thawing-out time. Evaluation of the concept during the first year of operation usually attempts to measure too many items. When this occurs, disappointment is likely because the results are not astounding. It is advisable to evaluate the effectiveness of the program piecemeal. For example, it might be wise to evaluate the program in terms of improved communication network and the beginning of trust relationships within the staff. For the next year the evaluating team may evaluate not only an improvement on these items, but improvement in terms of control and coordination as well. The author would like to stress here that evaluation should be made gradually and on a piecemeal basis in order to do justice to the program.

Question: What is so significant about the performance appraisal review session between the supervisor and the educator?

Answer: This is the occasion when the supervisor evaluates and coaches the educator on the basis of his performance achievement compared with objectives. The supervisor is interested in results obtained, not in the personality of the educator. The occasion is not used to chastise or reprimand for failure to achieve according to expectations. During this occasion the immediate supervisor will advise the educator in order to improve his performance. He will also offer his assistance in achieving the objectives. The significant difference between the traditional evaluation approach and the performance appraisal review via the School MBO program is that the emphasis is directed toward improving performance through counsel and assistance rather than through criticism and personality-catering, which have proved their ineffectiveness in the past.

Question: What is the most serious problem educators will encounter when implementing School MBO?

Answer: Experience has shown that there are two serious problems most school districts experience when implementing School MBO. First, there is a tendency for most school personnel to develop low-risk-bearing goals. Because of this, goal complacency sets in among the staff which produces negative overtones about the program. Administrators and supervisors must be on the alert to observe reactions towards goal-setting and must take immediate steps to combat mediocrity by seeking agreement to set more challenging goals. Low-risk-bearing goals generate low satisfaction. Secondly, administrators and supervisors are not yet trained in effective counseling, coaching techniques and adequate supervision, and assistance is not afforded educators in order to improve their performance. The result is that a considerable number of disgruntled educators complain about infrequent conferences with their immediate supervisors; too often there are insufficient recommendations and suggestions for improving performance with the program the scapegoat. To combat this, all supervisors must make provisions for frequent conferences with their educators. Workshops on effective counseling techniques should be instituted for all administrators and supervisors. Opportunities should also be afforded for consultants to sit in during the conference in an effort to assist them in improving their counseling techniques.

Appendix

Samples:

JOB DESCRIPTION

POSITION TITLE: Director of Art (K-12)

REPORTS TO: Assistant Superintendent for Instruction

BROAD FUNCTION: The director of art coordinates and supervises art and related activities at all educational levels throughout the district. He manages his department in such a way that its goals and objectives support and amplify those established by the Board of Education and the Superintendent of Schools for the district as a whole. To accomplish these ends, he continually develops and implements:

1. Capable art staffing.
2. Effective art programs which are responsive to the needs of students as well as to district-wide educational objectives, and which operate within the fiscal limitations established by the Board of Education.
3. Art-related activities designed to enrich specific school programs or to aid in the development of effective relationships with the community.

PRINCIPAL RESPONSIBILITIES: Within the approved limits of Board policy and administrative authority as delineated by the assistant superintendent for instruction, the art director is responsible for the following:

1. Staffing—Provide competent art teachers for district schools.
2. Organization—Arrange the scheduling of district art teachers to ensure that all schools receive adequate instructional service and advisory assistance in the area of the visual arts.
3. Curriculum—Develop and implement art programs which support district-wide educational goals and specific art-related objectives, and which meet state requirements for art education.
4. Supervision and Training—Observe, supervise, and evaluate the work of individual art teachers to ensure that art curriculum programs are actualized in an effective manner. Provide in-service training in art and related areas for art teachers and other district instructional personnel.
5. Supplies—Budget for, requisition, and provide adequate supplies for scheduled art programs and for art-related activities in other curriculum areas.
6. Facilities—Arrange for adequate facilities for conducting art

EXHIBIT A-1

programs and maintain an inventory of special equipment provided for this purpose.

7. Public Relations—Assist in the preparation of district publications.

8. Community Service—Inform the community regarding art activities in its schools and provide specific special programs for
community participation.

EXHIBIT A-1 (continued)

INDIVIDUAL IMPROVEMENT GUIDE

Patricia L. Galaska
ADMINISTRATOR / SUPERVISOR

Director of Art (k-12)
POSITION

July 10, 19--
DATE

BROOKS PUBLIC SCHOOLS

BROOKS, NEW YORK

EXHIBIT A-2

I. Main Purpose of Job
(State the main contribution of the job for the efficient operation of the school system)

Coordinate and supervise art and related activities at all educational levels throughout the district.

II. Position in Organization
    a.) Directly responsible to: Assistant Superintendent for Instruction

    b.) Staff directly supervised: art teachers (K-12)
    senior high art department chairman
    art department secretary

IV. Key Tasks

Key Area	Description of Key Task (main sub-division of the job)	Standard of Performance (results Targets)
1. S T A F F I N G	1.1 Provide competent art teachers for district schools. a. recruit art teachers	1.1a. N.Y. State certification. Minimum of 2 yrs' experience or observation of candidate's teaching ability in present position (or as guest in school district if not presently employed or doing student teaching)
	b. recruit substitute teachers in art	1.1b. N.Y. State certification

V. Personal Activities:
    (List those activities actually performed by you and not delegated. Items included here will be part of the Key Tasks)
    Provide staff and schedule art instructional personnel; develop art curriculum, supervise and evaluate art teachers; train and develop art staff; coordinate requisitioning and use of art supplies, equipment and facilities.

EXHIBIT A-2 (continued)

III. Scope of the Job
   (indicate your total responsibilites in terms of staff, materials and facilities)

Staff: 14 art teachers
           1 sr. high art dept. chrm.
           1 art dept. secretary

Facilities:
    4 elem. school art studios

Budget Allocation:

personnel (salaries	$164,000.
equipment (fan & kiln for 1 elem. school)	1,000.
supplies	9,000.
travel & conferences	500.

$174,500.

4 jr. high school art studios (2 with kilns)

3 sr. high school art studios (1 with kilns) plus art dept. office

1 art dept. office in central administration building

Method of Checking Performance	Suggestions for Performance Improvement
1.1a. Application; observation reports on in-service teachers; annual evaluation of teaching performance	1.1a. Endeavor to hire art teachers who were trained outside the metropolitan N.Y. area
1.1b. Assistant Superintendent for Instruction receives carbon copy of lists of available art substitutes sent to principals of individual schools	1.1b. Establish procedure for up-dating list of available substitute teachers in art annually

VI. Limits of Authority.
   (Items in this section will normally concern some or all of the following: physical resources, personnel and financial commitments.)

   Total budget for art supplies and equipment must not exceed $10,000; art teachers may be hired only upon collaboration with assistant superintendent for personnel and the principals of building in which they will serve; in-service course proposals must be approved by the district-wide "In-Service Committee."

EXHIBIT A-2 (continued)

IV. Key Tasks continued.

Key	Description of Key Task (main sub-division of the job)	Standard of Performance (results Targets)
2. O R G A N I Z A T I O N A L	2.1 Schedule assignments of district art teachers to individual schools.	2.1 Each school with a minimum of 25 instructional hours in art per week will have at least one full-time part teacher who does not travel to another building. Principals of respective schools agree to schedule assignment of art teachers to their building.
3. C U R R I C U L U M	3.1 Develop and implement art programs. a. Continually evaluate and up-date teaching guides used by art teachers K-12.	3.1a Bi-annual revision of curriculum guidelines for elementary art programs and for each art course at the secondary level. By 1980 all art curricula will be formulated in terms of behavioral objectives. All curricula will meet or exceed minimum N.Y. State requirements in art ed.
	b. Implement specific art curriculum guidelines in scheduled programs of art instruction.	3.1b Art teachers will use curriculum guidelines as a basis for their lesson plans.
	3.2 Aid in the development of art-related activities in other curriculum areas. a. Serve in a consultative capacity to principals and department chairmen seeking to develop art-related activities in their subject areas.	3.2a Art director meets with each school's principal (or assistant principal for instruction) and with the district director for each special subject area at least once annually to discuss the development of art-related activities for their areas of concern.
	b. Assist art teachers in planning art activities related to other curriculum areas.	3.2b Art director meets with each art teacher and selected department chairmen or grade leaders at least twice each year to participate in joint planning sessions.

EXHIBIT A-2 (continued)

Method of Checking Performance	Suggestions for Performance Improvement
2.1 Assistant Superintendent for Instruction receives copy of schedule of art teachers' assignments, initialed by principals of each school to indicate their agreement.	2.1 Make specific schedule for art teachers' advisory work and joint planning with teachers in other curriculum areas.
3.1a Review of revised curriculum guides as published.	3.1a In cooperation with students, develop a series of electives in art for students for the senior high "free" school.
3.1b Semi-annual review of art director's **written comments regarding art teachers'** plan books.	3.1b Establish procedure for getting regular feedback from teachers regarding usefulness of curriculum guides in art.
3.2a Meeting notices; copies of minutes of the meeting.	
3.2b Meeting notice; copy of minutes of the meeting.	

EXHIBIT A-2 (continued)

IV. **Key Tasks** continued.

Key Area	Description of Key Task (main sub-division of the job)	Standard of Performance (results Targets)
4. S U P E R V I S I O N	4.1 Observe the teaching performance of art staff.	4.1 The art director will make at least 3 formal observations of each art teacher annually. Observations will always involve post-observation conferences.
	4.2 Evaluate teaching performance and make recommendations regarding retention, dismissal, and appointment to tenure to principals of schools involved.	4.2 The teaching performance of all members of the instructional staff is to be evaluated annually. Teachers who fail to fulfill 50% or more of the objectives included in their individual improvement plans will not be retained. In cases where retention is recommended, the annual evaluation of teaching performance will culminate in the formulation of a new teacher's improvement plan for use in the forthcoming year.
	4.3 Communicate and interpret district policies and regulations to art staff and department secretary.	4.3 The art director will communicate district policies and regulations to his staff within 5 working days of his receipt of formal notification of such policies and/or regulations.

EXHIBIT A-2 (continued)

Method of Checking Performance	Suggestions for Performance Improvement
4.1 Observation reports Copies of notices setting time, date and place of post-observation conference.	4.1 Initiate use of pre-observation conference to further the process of counselling individual teachers regarding their professional objectives. Use video tape (or audio tape recordings) of lesson observed in post-observation conference.
4.2 Notice setting time, date and place of evaluation conference. Copy of recommendation regarding retention, dismissal or appointment to tenure forwarded to principals. Copy of individual improvement plan for the forthcoming year.	
4.3 Notice of meeting held to interpret policy or regulations, or written interpretation of policy sent to department staff.	

EXHIBIT A-2 (continued)

IV. Key Tasks continued.

Key Area	Description of Key Task (main sub-division of the job)	Standard of Performance (results Targets)
5. T R A I N I N G	5.1 Assist with district-wide orientation program	5.1 The art director will prepare an exhibit of representative student art work from both elementary and secondary levels for the orientation program. A presentation regarding regular art programs and special services available to teachers of subjects other than art will be given by the art director, at the request of the Asst. Supervisor for instruction, during regularly scheduled orientation meetings.
	5.2 Prepare a chapter for the District Teachers' Handbook outlining scheduled art programs and special services available to teachers in planning art-related activities.	5.2 The chapter will include a brief summary of course content for art classes in grades 1-8 and for each elective at the secondary level. Special services to non-art teachers for planning art-related activities will be comprehensively outlined and specific procedures for obtaining such assistance will be explained.
	5.3 Assist with district-wide conferences.	5.3 The art director will plan conference sessions and/or displays as requested by the Assistant Superintendent for instruction.
	5.4 Provide in-service training in art and related areas for art teachers and other district instructional personnel.	5.4 The art director will survey his dept. staff annually regarding in-service courses they would like to have offered. The art director, either independently or together with the director of another curriculum area or the principal of a school, will prepare and submit a proposal for an in-service course in his area at least one every year.
		5.5 Each teacher will spend at least one day out of every school year either in inter-school visitation or attending professional meetings. Funds required for registration fees and other expenses for professional meetings will not exceed appropriate budget allocations, ($500 for 19—)

EXHIBIT A-2 (continued)

Method of Checking Performance	Suggestions for Performance Improvement
5.1 Catalogue of exhibit. Asst. superintendent for instruction's written request for verbal presentation at orientation meeting. Orientation meeting program.	
5.2 District Teachers' Handbook	5.2 Include schedule of each art teacher's specifically scheduled times for advisory work with teachers of other subjects in chapter on art program.
5.3 Written request from asst. superintendent for instruction. Program for conference session or catalogue for display. Post-conference written report on conference session and/or display.	
5.4 Survey of art teachers' in-service course requests and art director's analysis of results. Copy of course proposal forwarded to district in-service committee. Copy of in-service committee's decision regarding course proposal. If the course is approved by in-service committee, record of teachers participating in course for in-service credit.	5.4 Consider requesting budget allocation to bring in in-service course instructors from outside the district (or to pay a district teacher who has a special area of expertise).
5.5 Teachers' requests for days for professional visitation and/or attendance at conferences. Teachers' requests for reimbursement for conference expenses.	

EXHIBIT A-2 (continued)

IV. Key Tasks continued

Key Area	Description of Key Task (main sub-division of the job)	Standard of Performance (results Targets)
5. T R A I N I N G	5.6 Call and conduct district-wide art department meetings on subjects of common interest. 5.7 Attend relevant conferences of and maintain membership in professional organizations.	5.6 The art dept. will meet as a whole at least twice annually. Each meeting should include provisions for participation presentations, or demonstrations from art teachers as well as from the art director. 5.7 The art director will be a member of the National Art Education Assoc., N.Y. State Art Teachers Assoc., Long Island Art Teachers Assoc. The art director will attend at least one relevant professional conference annually.
6. S U P P L I E S	6.1 Coordinate district-wide requisitioning of art supplies.	6.1 **A standardized bid sheet will be used** as the basis for art supply orders. The bid sheet will be revised every 5 years (or more often if teachers using it request such a revision). A maximum of 15% of the total budget code for consumable art supplies may **be ordered on a non-bid basis from** vendors specified by the teacher requesting said supplies. All preliminary art supply orders will be completed and in the hands of the asst. superintendent for business by March 15. Preliminary art supply orders will be revised if requested by the asst. superintendent for business. All purchase orders for consumable art supplies will be completed and in the hands of the asst. superintendent for business by May 15. Equitable distribution of consumable art supplies will be achieved by monitoring ordering on the basis of a per pupil cost for supplies. For 19-- each teacher may budget $2.50 per pupil for consumable art supplies.

EXHIBIT A-2 (continued)

Method of Checking Performance	Suggestions for Performance Improvement
5.6 Meeting notices. Copy of minutes of each meeting forwarded to asst. superintendent for Instruction.	
5.7 Membership cards. Request for day(s) to attend conference and (when applicable) application for reimbursement for conference expenses.	5.7 Attend conference of American Management Assoc., August 1-3, 19-- on P.P.B.S and its application to educational management.
6.1 Bid sheet Copies of bid sheet revisions. Copies of purchase orders for supplies ordered from vendors on a non-bid basis. Dated copy of preliminary art supply order. Written request from asst. superintendent for business specifying nature of revisions. Dated copies of purchase orders. Table analyzing and comparing per pupil supplies expenditures for the art department in each district school (prepared by art director).	6.1 Adjust per pupil supply allotments to differentiate between elementary, junior high and senior high art students, allowing proportionally higher per pupil expenditures for most costly supplies used in senior high elective art courses.

EXHIBIT A-2 (continued)

IV. Key Tasks continued.

Key Area	Description of Key Task (main sub-division of the job)	Standard of Performance (results Targets)
6. S U P P L I E S	6.2 Institute method of inventory control regarding art supplies available in each school building.	6.2 An inventory control book will be maintained for the art dept. of each school. This will include records of supplies on hand at the end of each school year, new supplies added and the date of their receipt, new totals for supplies on hand, a Feb. 1st check on quantities of supplies on hand, and a June 15th check on quantities of supplies on hand which will constitute the end of the year record of supplies on hand for the forthcoming year.
7. F A C I L I T I E S	7.1 Arrange for adequate facilities for conducting scheduled art programs in each school.	7.1 Each elementary art teacher assigned full time to a building will have a fully equipped art room. Peripatetic art teachers will be permitted the use of a special "art room" whenever possible. When this cannot be accomplished, they will have a steel utility cart with 2 shelves and a minimum surface area of 30" x 48" for their exclusive use whenever they are in the building. Each school will be equipped with a ceramic kiln of a minimum of 18" x 18" interior dimensions.
	7.2 Maintain an inventory of special equipment provided for use in art instruction.	7.2 An inventory sheet detailing the special equipment assigned for art instruction in each school will be filled out annually. Any discrepancies from equipment inventories of previous years (loss, replacement, etc.) will be duly noted with appropriate explanations.
	7.3 Arrange for necessary repairs and/or maintenance work of a special nature (beyond ordinary clearing) on art facilities and equipment.	7.3 Art director will inspect art facilities and special equipment for each school in April of each year to determine need for repairs, replacement or special maintenance work.

EXHIBIT A-2 (continued)

Method of Checking Performance	Suggestions for Performance Improvement
6.2 Art director's check of inventory books for each school in district. Art director's table of comparisons of supplies on hand in each school in June of each year.	6.2 Limit comparisons of supplies on hand to broad areas (e.g. construction paper, brushes, tempera paint, etc.) Use analysis of supplies on hand in June 19--, to aid teachers in ordering for 19--. **Investigate feasibility of transferring** portions of June inventory of supplies from one school to another so that they will be consumed more effectively.
7.1 Room assignments for each district school. Equipment inventory for each school. 7.2 Equipment inventory for each school. 7.3 Art director's report of equipment and facilities inspection.	

EXHIBIT A-2 (continued)

IV. Key Tasks continued.

Key Area	Description of Key Task (main sub-division of the job)	Standard of Performance (results Targets)
7. FACILITIES	7.4 Coordinate district-wide ordering of new equipment for art instruction.	7.4 Requests for equipment orders must be substantiated by detailed statement of need. All equipment orders for items over $50 in cost must go out for bids. All equipment orders must be in the hands of the assistant superintendent for business by May 15.
8. PUBLIC RELATIONS	8.1 Assist in preparation of district publications. a. Board of Education community newsletter b. Orientation booklet Curriculum guides in all subject areas.	8.1a Community Newsletter will be a minimum of 6 pages in length, with at least 3 illustrations, published 4 times annually. Photo offset printing done by high school print shop. 8.1b Orientation booklet will be a maximum of 50 pp. in length, with a maximum of 10 half-tone illustrations and an unlimited number of line drawings. Photo offset printing done by high school print shop. 8.1c Length and number of illustrations determined by content. 8 and 1/2 x 11 in. format bound in 3 ring binders to permit inexpensive revision. Art director will consult director of curriculum area in question when designing layout for curriculum guides. Photo offset printing by high school print shop.

EXHIBIT A-2 (continued)

Method of Checking Performance	Suggestions for Performance Improvement
7.4 Written requests for budget allocations for new equipment. Bid forms for all equipment over $50 in cost; purchase orders for all equipment under $50 in cost. Dated equipment orders.	
8.1a Copies of newsletter. Letters from citizens regarding news-letter. Enter newsletter in public relations contest sponsored by School Management Magazine. 8.1b Survey of new teachers regarding their use of orientation booklet. Copies of orientation booklet. 8.1c Copies of curriculum guides. Written approval of booklet design given by curriculum director of area covered in guide. Survey of teachers of each dept. (conducted a minimum of every 5 years) regarding lay-out, organization and content of their curriculum guides and their suggestions for improvement.	

EXHIBIT A-2 (continued)

IV. Key Tasks continued.

Key Area	Description of Key Task (main sub-division of the job)	Standard of Performance (results Targets)
9. C O M M U N I T Y S E R V I C E	9.1 Inform the community regarding art activities in its schools.	9.1 Art director will prepare an article on dept. activities for each issue of the Board of Education's Community Newsletter. The art director will speak with the Executive Board and/or the general membership of one school P.T.A. annually regarding art programs in that particular school.
	9.2 Provide special programs for community participation.	9.2 Each School's art dept. will participate in a minimum of one exhibit of student work annually. (The exhibit may be held in cooperation with the art dept. of another district school). The community will be invited to attend this exhibit. The art dept. will build sets for the senior high school's annual musical production. (The community may purchase tickets for this event.)

EXHIBIT A-2 (continued)

Method of Checking Performance	Suggestions for Performance Improvement
9.1 Community Newsletter as published. Meeting notice; minutes of the meeting noting art director's participation.	
9.2 Exhibit catalogues. Exhibit announcements circulated through-out the community. Program for the show and snapshots of sets and production as a whole forwarded to Assistant Superintendent for Instruction.	9.2 Develop art activities for recreation program being developed by community council against drug abuse.

EXHIBIT A-2 (continued)

SCHOOL/DEPARTMENT IMPROVEMENT PLAN

◁━━▷◁━━▷◁━━▷

SCHOOL/DEPARTMENT
Patricia L. Galaskas
ADMINISTRATOR/SUPERVISOR
Director of Art (K-12)
POSITION
July 10, 19--
DATE

BROOKS PUBLIC SCHOOLS

BROOKS, NEW YORK

EXHIBIT A-3

School/Department Improvement Plan

Date ___ July 10, _____ 19 _____

Area For Improvement	Problem (What's Wrong)	Objectives For Current Year	
		Main	Breakdown of Action
C U R R I C U L U M	Senior high "free" school was developed in 19--. "Free" school students have had no art electives. Students should be provided with opportunities to participate in existing art courses or they should have new art courses developed to suit their particular needs.	Together with "free" school students, to plan for their participation in existing art courses and/or to develop new elective courses for their special program by Oct. 31, 19--.	1. Meet with Mrs. Stanford, "free" school faculty advisor; get background on "free" school program and needs in terms of art program. 2. Meet with senior high art dept. chairman and committee of students from "free" school; arrive at proposals for specific art programs for "free" school. 3. Meet with art dept.; submit proposals for "free" school art programs for approval. 4. Meet with senior high art dept. chairman and committee of students from "free" school; discuss reactions to proposals and modify proposals if necessary. 5. Implement proposals. Arrange for placement of students with elementary art teachers as assistants, assign art teachers as advisors to students electing to do individual studio work, assign teacher for course entitled "Evaluating the Aesthetic Quality of our Environment." 6. Review programs. Meet with senior high art dept. chairman and committee of students from "free" school.

EXHIBIT A-3 (continued)

Administrator/Supervisor___Patricia L. Galaskas___

Position___Director of Art___

Target Date	Action By (Educator)	Outcome (Results, etc.)
August 31, 19--	Director of Art	On plan.
September 20, 19--	Director of Art	Amended-Meeting held Sept., 22 due to complications in "free" school schedule of activities.
October 5, 19--	Director of Art	On plan.
October 15, 19--	Director of Art	Below plan-Second meeting, held Oct., 20, needed to work out proposal modifications.
October 31, 19--	Director of Art	On plan-Student electing to do studio work in photography requested advisor from outside school system, local photographer was contacted and agreed to participate.
January 1, 19--	Director of Art	On plan.

EXHIBIT A-3 (continued)

School/Department Improvement Plan

Date _____ July 10, _____ 19 _____

Area For Improvement	Problem (What's Wrong)	Objectives For Current Year	
		Main	Breakdown of Action
C U R R I C U L U M	District teachers take advantage of special services for planning art related activities offered by art dept. at only about 10% level. This should be increased to a minimum of 50% of all district teachers participating in joint planning sessions with art teachers and/or art director.	To increase number of teachers participating in joint planning sessions with art teachers and/or directors to 50% of total district staff by June 31, 19--	7. Modify programs where necessary and implement modifications. 1. Request district art teachers to report on number of teachers who came to them for help in planning art related activities and total number of times each teacher participated in a joint planning conference. 2. Establish hypothesis regarding reasons for limited participation in joint planning conferences: a) analyze art teachers' schedules and reports on advisory work; b) meet with principals to discuss possible reasons for limited use of art teachers' advisory services. 3. Schedule 1 and 1/2 hours per week for art teachers to involve themselves in advisory work and joint planning sessions in meeting with principals. 4. Insure effective use of time scheduled for advisory services: a) meet with art teachers individually to discuss planning for use of time scheduled for advisory work and to set up schedule for joint planning conferences in which art director will participate (one for each art teacher in the Sept.-Jan. period); b) distribute

EXHIBIT A-3 (continued)

Administrator/Supervisor___Patricia L. Galaskas___

Position___Director of Art___

Target Date	Action By (Educator)	Outcome (Results, etc.)
March 30, 19--	Director of Art	Above plan-Completed by March 1, 19--
June 30, 19--	Director of Art	Below plan-Art teachers could not remember specific number of times they were consulted by each teacher. Amended to permit approximations in report.
August 15, 19--	Director of Art	Amended to use master schedules rather than art teachers' schedules which provide too little information. On plan, as amended.
August 31, 19--	Director of Art	On plan.
September 30, 19--	Director of Art	On plan.

EXHIBIT A-3 (continued)

School/Department Improvement Plan

Date __July 10,_____19_____

Area For Improvement	Problem (What's Wrong)	Objectives For Current Year	
		Main	Breakdown of Action
C U R R I C U L U M			memo to all district instructional personnel

Re: availability of art teachers' services for advice on relating art activities to their subject areas. Include specific schedule of art teachers' planning time.

5. Request that art teachers keep a record of teachers who consult them during scheduled planning time, number of consultations for each teacher, and number of teachers who request advisory services but can't come during planning time. Forward record to art director at end of each month.

6. Meet with art teachers, discuss pros and cons of scheduling plan time.

7. Evaluate results; analyze art teachers' monthly reports on use of planning time. |
| T R A I N I N G | 75% of district art teachers make only limited use of audio-visual aids in their teaching. Use of visual aids in art instruction should be increased so that 80% of district's art teachers use some | To increase use of audio-visual aids in art instruction so that 80% of district art teachers will be using some sort of visual aid in 60% of their lessons by June, 19-- | 1. Study situation. Review teachers' plan books for 19--

2. Get background information. Read Vincent Lanier, *Uses of Newer Media in Art Education* (NAEA, 1966). |

EXHIBIT A-3 (continued)

Administrator/Supervisor_____Patricia L. Galaskas_____

Position_____Director of Art_____

Target Date	Action By (Educator)	Outcome (Results, etc.)
November 1, 19--	Director of Art	On plan.
November 15, 19--	Director of Art	On plan-Art teachers find more teachers participating in joint planning since scheduled times were set.
June 30, 19--	Director of Art	On plan-50% of district teachers used advisory services, but participation was low as senior high. Further attention needed there.
August 31, 19--	Director of Art	On plan.
August 31, 19--	Director of Art	On plan.

EXHIBIT A-3 (continued)

School/Department Improvement Plan

Date ____July 10,_____19_____

Area For Improvement	Problem (What's Wrong)	Objectives For Current Year	
		Main	Breakdown of Action
T R A I N I N G	sort of visual aid in at least 60% of their lessons.		3. Begin to motivate interest in using A-V aids; conduct district art dept. meeting presenting research evidence on effectiveness of use of A-V aids, and have teachers who do use them tell why they find them helpful.
			4. Visit art teachers individually. Get information on the availability of "hardware" in each school and on individual teachers' levels of proficiency Re: use of hardward and production of software.
			5. Institute series of A-V workshops for art teachers on operation of machines and production of software for them.
			6. a) Conduct district art dept. meeting at which each teacher shows software he has made and others indicate if they would like a copy of it. b) Arrange to have copies made and distributed. Encourage teachers to share software they produced during workshop courses by permitting it to be duplicated.
			7. Evaluate results: review teachers' plan books to determine extent of use of A-V aids in presenting lessons.

EXHIBIT A-3 (continued)

Administrator/Supervisor___Patricia L. Galaskas___

Position___Director of Art___

Target Date	Action By (Educator)	Outcome (Results, etc.)
October 31 19—	Director of Art	On plan.
November 30 19—	Director of Art	Above plan—All teachers were visited by Nov. 15.
March 31 19—	Director of Art	Below plan—Teachers were preparing major exhibits of student work and suggested amending plan to eliminate session on opaque projector and tape recorders; art director agreed.
April 30, 19—	Director of Art	On plan.
June 30 19—	Director of Art	Below plan—There was a significant increase in the use of A-V aids. 90% of all district teachers are now using A-V aids in their teaching, but this was being done in only about 40% of their lessons. Still, this constituted marked improvement over the 19— level of 25% of teachers using A-V in 40% of their lessons.

EXHIBIT A-3 (continued)

School/Department Improvement Plan

Date ___July 10,_____19_____

Area For Improvement	Problem (What's Wrong)	Objectives For Current Year	
		Main	Breakdown of Action
S U P P L I E S	Elementary school principals have been ordering art supplies which classroom teachers do not use. Elementary art teachers receive numerous requests from classroom teachers for special art supplies. If these are distributed it hampers implementation of the art teacher's own program. Art supply ordering between general office (for classroom art supplies) and art dept. (for art class art supplies) needs to be coordinated.	To coordinate procedures for classroom art supply orders with art dept. art supply orders in all district elementary schools by January 31, 19--	1. Study situation. a) Study art dept. inventories dated June 30, 19-- b) request principal's office inventory of art supplies (June, 19--) for study; assemble notes from elementary art teachers complaining of receiving requests for art supplies from classroom teachers and make a list of specific supplies requested by classroom teachers in each school

2. Meet with building administrator and art teachers in each building to discuss ordering procedures and supply inventories on hand in June, 19--. Present analysis of problem to building principals and art teachers involved.

3. Meet with district art teachers to develop plan for coordinating classroom-art and art-art supply orders.

4. Marshal support for plan. Meet with building principals and present art dept. proposal RE: ordering of supplies. Point out advantages of having all art supply ordering centralized and burden this removes from clerks in the general office of the building

5. Implement plan; request that art teachers survey all teachers in each building Re: art supplies they anticipate using in 19-- |

EXHIBIT A-3 (continued)

Administrator/Supervisor___Patricia Galaskas_____

Position___Art Director_____

Target Date	Action By (Educator)	Outcome (Results, etc.)
August 15, 19--	Art Director	Delayed-Not all principals had accurate inventories of art supplies on hand in June, 19--, so art director offered to do inventory in these schools. Analysis was completed by Aug. 25.
Sept. 30, 19--	Art Director	On plan.
November 31, 19--	Art Director	On plan.
December 31, 19--	Art Director	On plan.
January 31, 19--	Art Director	On plan-All art teachers completed survey but not all classroom teachers could predict their supply needs for 19-- so art teachers will order for them.

EXHIBIT A-3 (continued)

School/Department Improvement Plan

Date ~~July 10,~~ _____ 19 _____

Area For Improvement	Problem (What's Wrong)	Objectives For Current Year	
		Main	Breakdown of Action
C O M M U N I T Y S E R V I C E	Board of Education passed policy regarding drug education program: Resolved that by 19—, a comprehensive drug education program will be instituted that will provide preventive as well as rehabilitative services. Director of Health Services, working together with Community Council Against Drug Abuse, plans to start evening recreation program for secondary school students. This program should include art activities.	To develop art-related activities for the evening recreation program by Nov. 15, 19—	1 Get background information on evening recreation program; a) meet with Dr. Green, district director of health services; b) attend a meeting of the Community Council Against Drug Abuse. 2. Formulate proposals; meet with secondary level art teachers and student members of Community Council Against Drug Abuse. 3. Attend joint meeting of district drug education planners and Community Council Against Drug Abuse. Submit proposals for approval. 4. Call Dr. Green to get joint committee's decision on proposals. 5. Implement program. Retain advisors, arrange for facilities, order supplies. 6. Conduct mid-year evaluation of program. Meet with directors of evening recreation program and a committee of participating students.

EXHIBIT A-3 (continued)

Administrator/Supervisor <u>Patricia Galaskas</u>

Position <u>Director of Art</u>

Target Date	Action By (Educator)	Outcome (Results, etc.)
August 31 19	Director of Art	On plan.
Sept. 20, 19--	Director of Art	On plan.
October 15, 19--	Director of Art	On plan.
October 30, 19--	Director of Art	Below plan-Amended to permit modification in proposed program suggested by adult members of Community Council Against Drug Abuse.
November 30, 19--	Director of Art	On plan.
February 1, 19	Director of Art	On plan-Teenagers have attended art related activities in recreation program regularly and request more adult supervision so groups can be enlarged to permit more to attend.

EXHIBIT A-3 (continued)

INDIVIDUAL IMPROVEMENT PLAN

Patricia L. Galaskas
ADMINISTRATOR / SUPERVISOR

Director of Art (K-12)
POSITION

July 10, 19--
DATE

BROOKS PUBLIC SCHOOLS

BROOKS, NEW YORK

EXHIBIT A-4

Individual Improvement Plan

Date <u>October 1,</u>____19_____

Key Area	Improvement Action (Objectives)	Step-by-Step Breakdown of Action Required
S T A F F I N G	To establish procedure for annual updating of list of available substitute teachers for art by November 30, 19--	1. Compile list of all art substitutes on file at each district school. 2. Send letter to placement bureau of local universities (Hofstra, Adelphi, Queens College, NYU, etc.) indicating that students or graduates with N.Y. State certification in art are invited to register as substitute teachers. 3. Review applications of substitute teacher candidates referred by universities and invite those with adequate credentials to come for interview. 4. Interview previously screened candidates and add names of those with adequate credentials to list of art substitutes. 5. Request principals and art teachers of each school to send a list of art substitutes they found inadequate to art director. (If all registered substitutes met performance standards for substitute teachers, teacher or principal should so indicate.) 6. Eliminate inadequate substitutes from list. 7. Contact all substitutes on amended list to ascertain their availability for substitute teaching assignments during the 19-- school year. 8. Compile complete list of art substitutes available for 19-- and forward copies of it to the principals of each district school.

EXHIBIT A-4 (continued)

Administrator/Supervisor _____ Patricia L. Galaskas_____

Position _____ Director of Art (K-12)_____

Target Date	By Whom	Outcome: (Results, delays, amendments)
Sept. 15, 19—	Mrs. Leonard (art dept. secretary)	On plan.
Sept. 30, 19—	Art director	On plan.
Sept. 30, 19—	Art director	On plan.
Oct. 31, 19—	Art director	Below plan—Delay, two candidates did not come for interviews until first week of November.
Sept. 30, 19—	Principals and art teachers	Below plan—New principal at Meadow School was unable to comment on quality of art substitutes; all other teachers and principals responded on schedule.
Oct. 15, 19—	Mrs. Leonard (secy)	On plan.
Nov. 15, 19—	Mrs. Leonard (secy)	Above plan—All individuals on list were contacted by November 6, 19—
Nov. 30, 19—	Mrs. Leonard (secy)	Above plan—Lists went out November 15th thanks to Mrs. Leonard, super secretary!

EXHIBIT A-4 (continued)

Individual Improvement Plan

Date __October 1__ 19 _____

Key Area	Improvement Action (Objectives)	Step-by-Step Breakdown of Action Required
O R G A N I Z A T I O N	To assign each district art teacher a specifically scheduled time period for use in advisory work and joint planning with teachers in other curriculum areas, by September 30, 19--	1.Analyze art teachers' 19-- class schedules and their reports RE: joint planning activities with teachers in other curriculum areas. Draw conclusions as to most effective scheduling of time for advisory work. 2.Meet with principal of each district school to discuss scheduling of a specific time for art teachers to devote to advisory work with teachers in other curriculum areas. Agree on a minimum of 1 and 1/2 hours per week for each art teacher and write time in on school's master schedule. 3.Distribute class schedules, including 1 and 1/2 hour specifically scheduled for advisory work, to district art teachers. 4.Meet individually with art teachers to discuss planning for effective use of time scheduled for advisory work. (Set up tentative schedule for art director's visits to assist in joint planning sessions with teachers in subject areas other than art.) 5.Distribute memo to all district instructional personnel RE: availability of art teachers' services for advice on art related activities and joint planning. Include specific schedule of art teachers' planning time in this memo. 6.Finalize schedule for art director's participation in joint planning session at each school for period Sept. -Jan. 30, 19-- 7.Follow-up: meet with art teachers to discuss pros and cons of specifically scheduled time for advisory work. Are more teachers participating in joint planning since there is a

EXHIBIT A-4 (continued)

Administrator/Supervisor ___Patricia L. Galaskas___

Position ___Director of Art___

Target Date	By Whom	Outcome: (Results, delays, amendments)
Aug. 15, 19--	Art director	Below plan-Art teachers' schedules alone did not provide sufficient information. Amended to include review of master schedule ot each school.
Aug. 31, 19--	Art director	On plan.
Sept. 10, 19--	Principals of respective schools	On plan.
Sept. 20, 19--	Art director	Below plan-Art director met with each teacher but not all art teachers were able to line up and arrive at dates for joint planning conferences.
Sept. 25, 19--	Art director	On plan.
Sept. 30, 19--	Art director	On plan.
Nov. 15, 19--	Art director	On plan-Art teachers find more teachers participate in joint planning since specifically scheduled time has been set for this. Consensus was the three periods of 1/2 hour each during the week was most practical arrangement

EXIIIBIT A-4 (continued)

Individual Improvement Plan

Date _____ 19 _____

Key Area	Improvement Action (Objectives)	Step-by-Step Breakdown of Action Required
		scheduled time for this? Is it more helpful to have one and 1/2 hours as one block of time or, e.g. as three shorter periods of time?
C U R R I C U L U M	To plan for participation of senior high "free" school students in existing art classes and/or to develop new art courses to suit their particular needs by October 31, 19--	1. Meet with Mrs. Stanford, advisor senior high "free" school, to get background information on the kind of art program students are interested in having. 2. Schedule meeting for art director and senior high art department chairman with committee of students from the "free" school to discuss nature of art program participation which will fulfill their needs. 3. Meet with students and senior high art department chairman to explore possibilities regarding art program for "free" school students. Outcome of this meeting should be a series of proposals regarding participation in existing art courses (nature, duration, etc.), and/or the development aesthetic quality of our environment, participation in art teaching at the elementary level, individual studio work in selected media, etc.) 4. Proposals arrived at in meeting with students are submitted to "free" school Board of Directors by students. 5. Proposals arrived at in meeting with students are submitted to a district-wide art dept. meeting to elicit art teachers' reactions and degree of support they are willing to lend. 6. Students, senior high art dept. chairman and art director meet to discuss reactions to proposals from "free" school Board of Directors and art dept. staff. Mrs. Stanford will be present at this meeting. Modifi-

EXHIBIT A-4 (continued)

Administrator/Supervisor ————————————————————————

Position ————————————————————————

Target Date	By Whom	Outcome: (Results, delays, amendments)
		for planning time.
Aug. 31, 19--	Art director	On plan.
Sept. 10, 19--	Art director	On plan.
Sept. 30, 19--	Art director	Amended-Meeting could not be held until Sept. 22 due to complications in "free" school schedule.
Sept. 30, 19--	Student representatives	On plan.
Oct. 5, 19--	Art director	On plan.
Oct. 15, 19--	Art director	Below plan-Second meeting needed to work out proposal nodifications, held Oct. 20.

EXHIBIT A-4 (continued)

Individual Improvement Plan

Date __October 1,__ 19 _____

Key Area	Improvement Action (Objectives)	Step-by-Step Breakdown of Action Required
		cations are made if necessary; plans for implementing proposals are finalized.
		7. Implement proposals.
		8. Meet with Mrs. Stanford and Board of Directors of "free" school to review art program devised for students and, where necessary, to outline modifications to be made.
		9. Discuss modifications with art dept. staff.
		10. Implement agreed upon modifications.
S U P E R V I S I O N	To initiate use of pre-observation conferences by Oct. 31, 19--	1. Meet with each district art teacher individually to counsel for setting objectives. Discuss use of pre-observation conference to aid in evaluating teachers' progress toward their own performance objectives.
		2. Request that each art teacher invite **art director to observe a** lesson during the month of October, 19--. (This may be done during conference for setting objectives, see #1 above.)
		3. Confirm date for lesson observation during October and schedule a pre-observation conference to be held 2-5 school days before the observation.
		4. Conduct pre-observation conference and lesson observation for each district art teacher.
		5. Conduct post-observation conference for October lesson observation. At this conference, elicit teachers' reactions to and opinion of value of pre-observation conference.

EXHIBIT A-4 (continued)

Administrator/Supervisor _____

Position _____

Target Date	By Whom	Outcome: (Results, delays, amendments)
October 31, 19--	Art director and Mrs. Stanford	On plan.
January 31, 19--	Art director	On plan.
February 28, 19--	Art director	Above plan-Completed by Feb. 15, 19--
March 30, 19--	Art director	Above plan-Completed by March 1, 19--
Sept. 30, 19--	Art director	On plan.
Sept. 30, 19--	Art director	On plan.
Oct. 5, 19--	Art director	Below plan-Because of conflicts between times teachers invited art director to observe, scheduling was not completed until Oct. 10, 19--
Oct. 31, 19--	Art director	Below plan-One teacher's pre-observation conference and lesson observation was done during first of November.
Nov. 15, 19--	Art director	On plan-Teachers found pre-observation conferences helpful in clarifying their objectives and constructing unit plans which supported their long-range goals.

EXHIBIT A-4 (continued)

Individual Improvement Plan

Date <u>October 1,</u> 19 _____

Key Area	Improvement Action (Objectives)	Step-by-Step Breakdown of Action Required
T R A I N I N G	To increase district art teachers' use of audio-visual aids so that 80% of district art teachers will use visual aids in at least 60% of their lessons by June 13, 19--	1. Study 19-- plan books for record of teachers' use of audio-visual aids in their instruction. 2. Read: Vincent Lanier, <u>Uses of Newer Media in Art Education</u> (NAEA, 1966). 3. Schedule art dept. meeting on topic of using A-V aids. Art director should present research documenting effectiveness of such aids in teaching art. The 25% of district art teachers presently using A-V aids regularly should make a brief presentation regarding their reasons for using these aids and the impact they feel A-V aids have on their lessons. 4. Visit art dept. teachers individually to discuss availability of A-V equipment in their schools and their ability to operate the equipment and prepare their own "software" for use with the equipment. 5. Institute a series of A-V workshop on: a) operating overhead projector and making transparencies b) operating 16mm. movie projector and locating inexpensive film resources (Nassau Library System, local companies, rental catalogues, etc.) c) operating 35mm. slide projector and photographing illustrations from art books to use in slide presentations d) operating the filmstrip projector and drawing your own filmstrips (include also: information on filmstrips available in the district and free of charge from the Nassau Library system) e) operating the super 8mm. loop projector and making your own super 8mm. movies and loops f) operating the opaque projector and tape recorders (reel to reel and cassette)

EXHIBIT A-4 (continued)

Administrator/Supervisor <u>Patricia L. Galaskas</u>

Position <u>Art Director</u>

Target Date	By Whom	Outcome: (Results, delays, amendments)
August 31, 19--	Art director	On plan.
August 31, 19--	Art director	On plan.
October 31, 19--	Art director (and teachers using A-V aids to make presentations)	
November 30, 19--	Art director	Above plan-Teachers were all visited by November 15.
March 31, 19--	Art director	Amended-Teachers were preparing major exhibits of student work and suggested eliminating session on opaque projector and tape recorders; art director agreed.

EXHIBIT A-4 (continued)

Individual Improvement Plan

Date <u>October 1,</u> 19 _____

Key Area	Improvement Action (Objectives)	Step-by-Step Breakdown of Action Required
		6. Schedule art dept. meeting for teachers to show the "software" they have made during the workshops for use in their own courses. Where possible, arrange to copy individual teacher's materials for any other teacher who would find them useful. 7. Review plan books to determine extent of use of A-V aids in presenting lessons.
C O M M U N I T Y S E R V I C E	**To develop art related activities** for the evening recreation program sponsored by the district drug education program and the Community Council Against Drug Abuse by Nov. 15, 19--	1. Meet with Dr. Green, director of health services, to get background information on specific objectives of evening recreation program and details regarding proposed organization. 2. Attend meeting of Community Council Against Drug Abuse for information on purpose, organization, and funding of evening recreation program. 3. Meet with secondary level art teachers and student members of Community Council Against Drug Abuse to formulate specific proposals for art related activities to be included in recreation program (e.g. open ceramics studio, filmmaking, painting, film study using low-cost rental films, etc.). 4. Attend joint meeting of district drug education program planners and Community Council Against Drug Abuse to submit program proposals for approval. 5. Get approval for proposals. 6. Implement program (hire advisors, locate facilities, order supplies, etc.). 7. Conduct mid-year evaluation of success of program.

EXHIBIT A-4 (continued)

Administrator/Supervisor _Patricia L. Galaskas_

Position _Director of Art_

Target Date	By Whom	Outcome: (Results, delays, amendments)
April 30, 19--	Art director	On plan.
June 30, 19--	Art director	Below-plan—There was a significant increase in the use of A-V aids. 95% of all district art teachers were now using A-V aids in their teaching but this was done in only about 40% of their lessons. Improvement plan for 19-- will concentrate upon improving frequency of use of A-V aids.
August 15, 19--	Art director	On plan.
August 31, 19--	Art director	On plan.
Sept. 30, 19--	Art director	On plan.
Oct. 15, 19--	Art director	On plan.
Oct. 30, 19--	Art director	Below plan-Amended to permit modification in proposed program suggested by adult members of Community Council Against Drug Abuse and agreed to by students and art director.
Nov. 30, 19--	Art director	On plan.
Feb . 1, 19--	Art director, director of evening recreation program and committee of students participating in program	On plan-Teenagers have attended art related activities in program regularly and request more adult supervision so that groups can be enlarged to permit more to attend.

EXHIBIT A-4 (continued)

Bibliography

From 1970 to Present

Armstrong, Robert J.; Corne, Terry D.; Kramer, Robert E.; Robertson, E. Wayne, *A Scheme for Management by Objectives*, Educational Innovators' Press, Tucson, Arizona, 1972.

Armstrong, Robert J.; Corne, Terry D., Kramer, Robert E., Robertson, E. Wayne, *Implementing Management by Objectives*, Educational Innovators' Press, Tucson, Arizona, 1973.

Carroll, Stephen J., and Tosi, Henry L., Jr., *Management by Objectives--Application and Research*, The MacMillan Company, New York, N.Y., 1973.

Dyer, Frederick D., and Dyer, John M., *The Enjoyment of Management*, Dow, Jones-Irwin, Inc., Homewood, Illinois, 1971.

Hacker, Thorne, "Management by Objectives for School," Administrator's Notebook—Mid West Administration Center, The University of Chicago, Vol. XX, November 1971, No. 3.

Lewis, James, Jr., *Appraising Teacher Performance*, Parker Publishing Co., Inc., West Nyack, N.Y., 1973.

Mali, Paul, Management by Objectives—*An Operating Guide to Foster and More Profitable Results*, Interscience, New York, N.Y., 1972.

Whritner, John A., and Antin, Arthur P., *Program Planning--Using Management by Objectives in School Administration*, Prentice-Hall, Inc., Englewood Cliffs, N.J., 1972.

From 1960 to 1969

Ansoff, H.I., "Company Objectives: Blueprint or Blue Sky?" *Management Review* (September, 1962).

Batten, J.D., "Beyond Management by Objectives," American Management Association, New York, 1966.

Bittel, Lester R., *Management by Exception: Systemizing and Simplifying the Managerial Job*, McGraw-Hill, New York, 1964.

Calhoun, Richard P., and Kirkpatrick, C.S., *Technique of Successful Supervision*, Prentice-Hall, Inc., Englewood Cliffs, N.J., 1960.

Drucker, Peter V., *Managing for Results: Economic Tasks and Risks–Making Decisions*, Heinemann, London, 1964.

Forrest, Andrew, "Manager's Guide to Setting Targets," Industrial Society (Notes for Managers No. 10), London, 1966.

Gellerman, Saul W., "Management by Motivation," American Management Association, 1968.

Glickman, Albert S.; Hahn, Clifford P.; Fleishman, Edwin A., Baxter, Brent, *Top Management Development and Succession: An Exploratory Study*, Macmillan, New York; Collier-Macmillan, London, 1968.

Granger, Charles H., "The Hierarchy of Objectives," *Harvard Business Review*, May-June, 1964.

Hoppock, Robert, "Ground Rules for Appraisal Interviewers," *Personnel*, May-June, 1961.

Howell, R.A., "Fresh Look at Management by Objectives," *Business Horizons*, 10 (fall 1967).

Hughes, Charles L., "Goal Setting: Key to Individual and Organizational Effectiveness," American Management Association, New York, 1965.

Humble, John W., *Improving Business Results*, McGraw-Hill Publishing Company Limited, Maidenhead, Berkshire, England, 1968.

Humble, J.W., "Improving Management Performance," Management Publications for the British Institute of Management, rev. ed., London, 1969.

Huston, C.L., "Setting Corporate Objectives," *Duns Review* and *Modern Industry* (October, 1969).

Kellogg, Marion S., "Closing the Performance Gap: Results-Centered Employee Development," American Management Association, New York, 1967.

Likert, Tensis, *The Human Organization: Its Management and Value*, McGraw-Hill, New York and London, 1967.

MacConkey, Dale D., "How to Manage by Results," American Management Association, New York, 1965.

McGregor, Douglas, *The Human Side of Enterprise*, McGraw-Hill, New York, 1960.

Miller, Ernest C., "Objectives and Standards: An Approach to Planning and Control," American Management Association (AMA Research Study 87), 1967.

National Industrial Conference Board, "Developing Managerial Competence: Changing Concepts, Emerging Practices," New York, 1964.

Odiorne, G.S., *Management by Objectives: A System of Managerial Leadership*, Pitman, New York, 1965.

Odiorne, George S., *Management Decisions by Objective*, Prentice-Hall, Inc., Englewood Cliffs, N.J., 1969.

Schaffer, Robert H., "Management by Total Objectives," (Management Bulletin No. 52), American Management Association, General Management Division, New York, 1964.

Scheild, Phil N., "Charter of Accountability for Executives," *Harvard Business Review*, July-August, 1965.

Schleh, Edward C., *Management by Results: The Dynamics of Profitable Management*, McGraw-Hill, New York, 1961.

Stull, Richard Allen, "Determining Management Objectives," Rydges, April, 1963.

Stumpf, Charles F., "Administration by Objectives," Hostibal Administration, 6, (winter 1961), 43-50.

Valentine, Raymond F., "Appraisal Interviewing Without Stress or Strain," *Supervisory Management*, December, 1965.

Valentine, Raymond F., "Laying the Groundwork for Goal Setting," *Personnel*, January-February, 1966.

Valentine, Raymond F., "Performance Objectives for Managers," American Management Association, New York, 1966.

Warren, Malcolm W., *Training for Results: A Systems Approach to the Development of Human Resources in Industry*, Addison-Wesley Publishing Company, Reading, Mass., 1969.

Wickert, F.R., and McFarland, D.E., *Measuring Executive Effectiveness*, Appleton-Century-Crofts, New York, 1967.

Wickstrom, Walter S., "Management by Objectives or Appraisal by Results," *The Conference Board Record*, July, 1966.

From 1950 to 1959

Drucker, Peter F., *The Practice of Management*, Heinemann, London, 1955.

Mahler, Walter R., "Bringing About Change in Individual Performance," General Management Series 186, American Management Association, New York, 1957.

Index